KNITTING WITH BALLS

A hands-on guide to knitting for the MODERN MAN

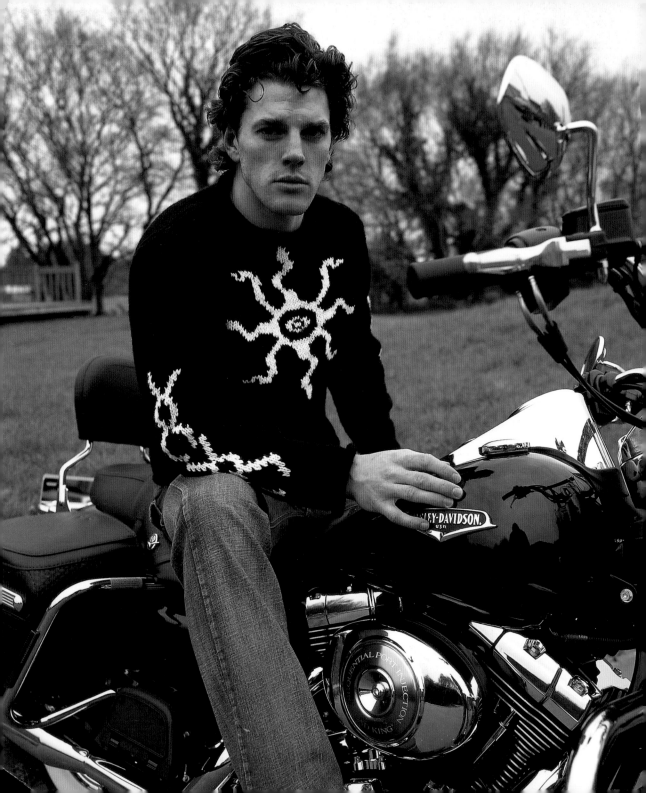

KNITTING WITH BALLS

A hands-on guide to knitting for the
MODERN MAN

Michael del Vecchio

London, New York, Munich, Melbourne, Delhi

First published in the United States by
DK Publishing, 375 Hudson Street,
New York, New York 10014.

Publisher Carl Raymond
Executive Managing Editor Sharon Lucas
Editor Nichole Morford
Art Director Dirk Kaufman
Managing Art Editor Michelle Baxter
Production Manager Ivor Parker
Creative Consultant John Brinegar

A CIP catalog record for this book is available
from the Library of Congress

ISBN-13: 978-0-7566-2289-3
ISBN-10: 0-7566-2289-1

Printed and bound in China.
05 06 07 08 09 10 9 8 7 6 5 4 3 2 1

This book was conceived, designed, and produced by
IVY PRESS LIMITED
The Old Candlemakers
West Street, Lewes
East Sussex BN7 2NZ, UK

Creative Director Peter Bridgewater
Publisher Jason Hook
Editorial Director Caroline Earle
Art Director Sarah Howerd
Senior Project Editor Emily Gibson
Technical Editors Karen Frisa, Witt Pratt
Designer Joanna Clinch
Photographers Ivan Jones and Calvey Taylor-Haw
Illustrator Peters & Zabransky
Models Amanda, Moshe, Sam, and Willis from Nevs, London
Knitted Samples Marney Andersen, Molly Bettridge,
Christine Cornwell, Holly Daymude, Courtney Messenger,
Genia Planck, Witt Pratt, Michael del Vecchio

For more information about Ivy Press Ltd,
go to www.ivy-group.co.uk

Discover more at www.dk.com

Contents

Introduction 6

Tools, Materials, Basics 9

Accessories 29

Sweaters & Jackets 77

Home Gear 125

Customizing Patterns & Knitting Resources 143

Index & Acknowledgments 158

Introduction

Since I started knitting in the spring of 2001—when my friend Charles invited Dawn over to his house and she taught us both—I have had more than a few opportunities to study why men knit and how we fit into the "chain" of the craft. Across the United States, and farther out into the world, there are countless male knitters coming from every walk of life and knitting for all sorts of reasons.

above Joining a knitting club is a great way to feel at home with your knitting. Improve your skills and exchange information with like-minded knitters. Some knitting circles are aimed specifically at guys. Use our resource guide (see page 152), the internet, or local listings in magazines to track down one in your neighborhood.

At Waldorf schools (based on the teaching of Rudolf Steiner), all students—male and female—are taught to knit at a young age before even learning to read or write, because knitting develops hand–eye coordination, helps students follow instructions, and gives them a sense of satisfaction and self-esteem. At Knit NY (a yarn store in New York City), men's knit nights are held weekly, and a storeful of guys show up to practice their knits and purls, share stories, and gather as a community. The evidence is clear: in stores, in schools, and at home, men are knitting in full force.

Difficulty Rating

The level of difficulty is shown above the heading for each project.

● ○ ○ JUST RIGHT FOR BEGINNING KNITTERS

● ● ○ IDEAL FOR INTERMEDIATE KNITTERS

● ● ● DESIGNED FOR ADVANCED KNITTERS

What's more, they have been doing so for centuries. *Knitting with Balls* is full of examples of men in the history of knitting and fiber-related craft. It is also full of great modern designs. Within its pages you will find twenty-two projects for the male knitter to make for himself—and for men and women to knit for their partners, husbands, and other male relatives and friends. It includes seven sweaters, vests, and jackets that illustrate the current styles in menswear; eleven accessories, including cozies, socks, and scarves; and four projects for the home, ranging from a utility cloth to a travel bag—all designed with the modern male in mind.

At the end of the book, I devote a full chapter to the structure of garments, with detailed instructions on how to alter and design your own patterns: everything from inspiration to stitch selection to the use of color.

This book is here to prove those people wrong who talk about knitting not being a *proper hobby for boys*. Today many people feel that men don't knit, never have, and ultimately shouldn't, because knitting is part of "the woman's domain." To my mind, the fact that men are knitting, and have always knit, is part of what makes the craft so cool and, in some respects, so *revolutionary*.

Gentlemen, take up your needles!

Knitting landmarks

The twentieth century was marked by more than a few notable milestones in the realm of men's knitting and garment design.

- In 1946 James Norbury became Chief Designer for Patons, a manufacturer of yarn in the United Kingdom. During his lifetime he published several knitting pattern books— and had his own television show.

- In 1969 Kaffe Fassett—known for his rich use of color—published his first pattern in an issue of *Vogue Knitting*: the Moroccan Waistcoat. Today Fassett is widely respected for the contributions he makes to unisex and male-only garments in knitting.

- In 1972 Dave Fougner wrote *The Manly Art of Knitting*, a sixty-four-page booklet (now out of print). The patterns included a dog blanket, a set of saddlebags, and a hammock knitted using shovel handles or billiard cues.

- In 1982 Hashimoto Osanu published *Chiyareji Nitto: Otoka Amu* (Knitting Challenge: Men Too Can Knit), a beginners' style book. It contained four basic sweaters for men; a second book was released in 1983 with variations.

- In 1987 Richard Rutt published *A History of Hand Knitting*, the first complete and accurate account of the craft.

A brief history of men in knitting

Before I launch into the contributions that men have made to the world of knitting, it should be noted that the roots and development of the craft are vague and diverse. Knitting evolved—often simultaneously—in South America, Europe, North America, and beyond. People knit because they were poor (and cold), and the politics of gender had little to do with it.

Disclaimer aside, knitting first traveled to Europe at the end of the first millennium via sailors aboard fishing boats from the Middle East. Later, knitting guilds (initially male-only) were formed in Europe in the sixteenth century. To successfully attain status within the guild, knitters were required to complete a minimum of six years' training; large projects (such as an eight- by twelve-foot knitted rug) marked their progress up the ranks.

Since then men have been responsible for countless fiber-related inventions. In England in 1589 Reverend William Lee invented the knitting machine, designed initially to make a flat stockinette fabric. A patent was eventually issued to Lee in France, after Elizabeth I feared that the machine would drastically change the economic scene in England (which it later did). The machine was subsequently improved upon by Jedediah Strutt, who developed a device to add ribbing to garments, and by Marc Brunel, who in the nineteenth century developed a machine that would knit in the round.

In the late eighteenth century Eli Whitney invented the Cotton Gin machine to process cotton more effectively and speedily. In the mid-nineteenth century John Mercer found that treating cotton with a strong caustic soda would *mercerize* it—thus making it more absorbent, lustrous, and durable. Around the same time, Count Hilaire de Chardonnet used an extract of mulberry leaves to form an artificial silk: the first rayon.

Recently, the link between men and knitting has been pulled in many new directions. During the two World Wars men knit both at war and while recovering in the hospital. Male surgeons began knitting in the twentieth century because the handiwork helped to keep their fingers from getting stiff. And out west—even today—it's not uncommon to find men knitting socks while tending their cattle. Looking forward, as more and more men are learning this wonderful craft, the community is growing and men may once again be the principal group of craftsters.

Tools
Materials
Basics

Tools

Any good handyman knows you can't do the job without the right tools! Double-pointed needles, stitch markers, row counters—the best way to get to know these items and what they do is to start working with them. In the meantime, here are a few hints on what's what.

Knitting needles

Straight knitting needles Straight, single-pointed needles, ranging in length from eight to sixteen inches. They're great for any small project you want to work back and forth.

Circular knitting needles Two short, straight needles connected by a long piece of plastic or wire. Ranging in length from eight inches up to sixty inches, they are better suited to projects that require a large surface area and can be used to knit garments in the round.

Double-pointed needles Sets of four or five short needles, each having two points. Ranging in length from five to ten inches, double-pointed needles also enable the user to work in the round, but with more control over smaller surface areas. They are necessary for small projects such as mittens and socks.

Notions

Nylon tape measure Essential for measuring gauge and the length of your knitted piece.

Cable needle A double-pointed needle with a crook or turn in it used to create a cable—or a series of twists and crossovers—in knitting.

Stitch markers Little rings made of plastic, metal, or rubber, used to help mark changes in stitch, increases, decreases, or the start of a round on a garment. Use rubber washers, jump rings, or nuts as stitch markers if you find yourself in need without a yarn store in sight.

Row counter Helps you keep track of the number of rows worked in a piece.

Tapestry needle Also known as a yarn or darning needle, a tapestry needle is a long sewing needle with an eye large enough to accommodate yarn and a blunt end. It is most

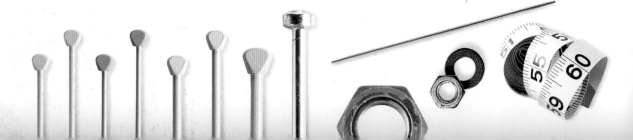

often used for weaving in your ends, but is also necessary for sewing together seams.

Stitch holder A large safety pin, often used in garments such as sweaters, where sleeve or shoulder stitches may need to be put on hold.

Safety pins An essential tool for finishing, safety pins hold your knitted pieces in place while you sew them together.

Scissors / yarn cutter While most yarns can be pulled apart or broken between your fingers, some can't. Keep a yarn cutter or a pair of small, sharp scissors with you to reduce those painful cuts to your fingers.

Yarns

When choosing yarn for a project, bear in mind that its gauge will affect stitch size and overall feel of the fabric (see page 25). Here's a quick 101 on the basics of yarn weights:

Super bulky A yarn that yields a gauge of up to 2.5 stitches per inch. This thick and bulky yarn is ideal for quick knits such as scarves.

Bulky A yarn that typically yields a gauge of three to 3.75 stitches per inch. Bulky yarn

will make a great first sweater (because it's quick) and is ideal for scarves and hats. Bulky and super bulky yarn won't knit tightly, so the resulting fabric may not be as impenetrable to cold wind, rain, or snow as one in a finer wool.

Worsted Divided into two classes—heavy worsted (often known as Aran) and light worsted—worsted weight yarn yields a gauge of 3.75 to five stitches per inch and is ideal for a wide range of projects.

Double knitting (DK) A yarn that yields a gauge of five to six stitches per inch, and is most commonly used for sweaters, socks, and mittens. DK yarns make a smaller stitch and offer more opportunity to use textured stitches and color.

Fingering A lightweight yarn that yields a gauge of six to eight stitches per inch. It is ideal for socks and projects with detailed colorwork.

Lace Yielding a gauge of more than eight stitches per inch, lace weight yarns are delicate and wispy, and are perfect for open items such as shawls and scarves.

Reading a yarn label

It's not unusual to feel a bit lost the first time you enter a yarn store. Your first step? Pick up a ball of yarn and look at the information on the label. Then, use this breakdown of our fictitious label to help you decipher it. If you're still lost, ask the people who work there: they live to talk yarn!

■ The name of the company that produces the yarn.

■ The name of the yarn.

■ The yarn composition. It's especially important to look at this when knitting for people who are sensitive to wool, angora, or scratchy fibers. Here the information is offered in different languages.

■ A note found only on yarns from the United Kingdom, B.S. 984 is a British Standard that regulates the temperature and humidity of the yarn as it's being packaged, so that the buyer can be certain that the length and weight of the yarn is uniform from ball to ball.

■ The length of yarn in the ball you're holding. This is especially useful information when substituting one yarn for another in a pattern.

■ The shade number. Shade numbers prevent the buyer from confusing two or more similar colorways. Shade is synonymous with color.

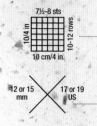

7½–8 sts

10/4 in

10–12 rows

10 cm/4 in.

12 or 15 mm   17 or 19 US

GUY WOOL

guy big wool

100% MERINO WOOL
100% MERINO WOLLE
100% MERINO LAINE

100g

In accordance with B.S. 984
Approx Length 80m (87 yards)

www.guywool.com

SHADE   LOT

28   16478

Hand wash

Warm iron

Do not bleach

Dry clean in certain solvents

Do not tumble dry
Dry flat out of direct sunlight

This grid tells you that if you use the suggested needle size, in this case a US size 17 or 19 (12 or 15 mm), you should get 7½–8 stitches to 4 in./10 cm, in stockinette stitch, at a normal tension. When substituting yarns, be sure that the information on this grid is similar (if not the same). See the description of gauge on page 25, for more information on what gauge is and why it's important.

This symbol tells you that this yarn is best knit on US size 17 or 19 (12 or 15 mm) needles. It also relates to the gauge (see page 25).

The weight of the ball you're holding.

The yarn company's website. Check it out to view their complete line, new yarns, and other colorways available for each yarn.

The dyelot. Yarn is dyed in batches, and the lot numbers (or batch numbers) change from batch to batch. When purchasing yarn for a project, make sure you're buying enough balls to complete it—and that they all have the same lot number, to avoid unintentional stripes in your project.

These symbols indicate how the finished garment should be cared for. Considering the care of a garment is important—especially when choosing yarns for items that will become a gift.

How to make a slip knot

Any good Boy Scout should remember how to make a slip knot if he earned the merit badge in knot tying. In knitting, the slip knot is used as the preparatory stitch to casting on. When counting your cast-on stitches, the slip knot counts as the first stitch.

1. Unwrap a few yards of yarn from your ball and drape the cut edge of the yarn over the front of your left hand. Reach around to the yarn falling down the back of your hand and wrap it clockwise around your index and middle finger, holding the two strands loosely with your index finger and thumb. Insert the tip of a knitting needle, held in your right hand, into the loop and pull a strand of yarn through.

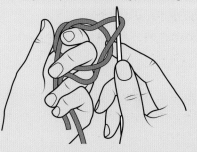

2. Continue pulling the needle and strand of yarn up and away from the left hand. Remove your left index and middle fingers from the wrapped yarn, and pull the two strands of yarn hanging from the knot to tighten.

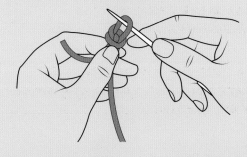

Long-tail cast-on

The long-tail cast-on (also referred to as the double cast-on) is a great technique for beginners. It's sturdy, secure, and especially good for garments that need a bit of stretch on the edges, such as hats, socks, and mittens.

Tip

As you become more comfortable with the long-tail cast-on, you may choose to work this cast-on using only one needle instead of two, to create a more subtle edge.

1. Begin by taking both needles together and wrapping the yarn around both for the number of stitches you'll be casting on. For example, to cast on thirty stitches, wrap the yarn around the needles thirty times. From the point where you stop wrapping, measure out another ten inches or so of extra yarn.

3. At the same time, pinch together the thumb and index finger of your left hand. Insert them between the two pieces of yarn falling from the slip knot on the right-hand needle and spread them open. The end of the yarn that's attached to the ball should be over your thumb.

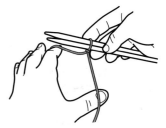

2. There, make your slip knot (see page 13) and unravel the yarn you've wrapped around the needle. Insert the needle through the slip knot, then tighten it around the needle.

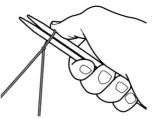

4. With the third, fourth, and fifth fingers of your left hand, grab the two pieces of yarn hanging down from your thumb and index finger. You should see a diamond shape when you pivot your left hand toward you.

5. Using this setup, insert the tip of the needle under the piece of yarn coming down off your thumb, through the gap created by the two lengths of yarn.

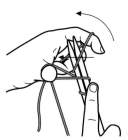

6. Then, bring the needle over the piece of yarn twisted around the index finger and through the gap created by the two lengths.

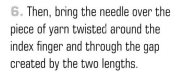

7. End by bringing the needle back down through the gap created by the piece of yarn wrapped around your thumb.

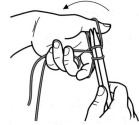

8. Let go with your left hand and pull on the two pieces of yarn to secure the stitch. Begin the setup again from step 4 for each of the required number of stitches.

When the required number of stitches has been cast on, remove one needle if you've casted on over two, and begin to work your first row. Remember: when counting stitches, your slipknot counts as one stitch.

Cable cast-on

The cable cast-on, a knitted cast-on worked by inserting the right-hand needle in between two loops on your left-hand needle, is perfect for any garment that needs a finished edge. For the edge of a sweater, scarf, shawl, or wallet, the cable cast-on holds your stitches securely in place, but won't ever stretch. Once you know how to knit, the cable cast-on is a breeze.

Tip

The trick to a successful cable cast-on is to wait to tighten the yarn until after the right-hand needle is back in between the two stitches, ready to grab more yarn. If you tighten the yarn beforehand, the stitches will be too tight to get the needle in between.

1. Place a slip knot snugly on the left-hand needle. Insert the tip of the right-hand needle under the left and into the knot to form an X.

2. Hold the two needles together with your left thumb and index finger. Then, with your right hand, wrap the yarn around the needle from the right hand—bringing it under the right-hand needle and then back over, counterclockwise.

3. Inch the right-hand needle and the yarn wrapped around it out of the slip knot. Continue to hold on to the slip knot with your left index finger.

4. Now pull the right-hand needle toward you, and put the stitch directly onto the left-hand needle (do not twist it). You now have two stitches.

5. For the next stitch, and every subsequent stitch, reinsert the right-hand needle, this time in between the two stitches on the needle. Wrap the yarn around the needle in the same way, and repeat steps 3 and 4.

Holding the yarn

There are two main camps on how to hold the yarn when knitting: English style and Continental. Both styles involve wrapping the yarn around two fingers to help control the tension, and both styles have their pros and cons. However, when you're just starting out and getting used to all the steps involved in making a stitch, it's also OK to pick up and drop the yarn every time you need it. Later, you can choose which style of holding the yarn is most comfortable for you.

English (or American) style

Knitters who knit English style are often termed "throwers," based on how the yarn gets "thrown" around the needle. To hold the yarn English style:

1. Wrap the yarn first around your little finger and then around your index finger on your right hand.

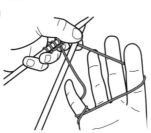

2. When holding the yarn English style while you knit, be sure to stretch the right index finger upward a bit, to help control the tension in your stitches.

Continental (or German) style

Knitters who knit Continental style are often termed "pickers," because the yarn is picked up by the needle each time you knit or purl a stitch. To hold the yarn Continental style:

1. Wrap the yarn first around your little finger and then around your index finger on your left hand.

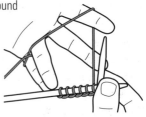

2. When holding the yarn Continental style while you knit, be sure to stretch your left index finger upward a bit to help control the tension in your stitches and to make it easier to "pick" the yarn.

Holding the yarn English style

Most knitters will tell you they learned to knit English style first. The main benefit is that it allows knitters who are typically right-handed the opportunity to use their dominant hand to do the majority of the work.

Knitting

To begin knitting English style, first cast on a few stitches using either the long-tail cast-on or cable cast-on method (see pages 14 and 16).

1. Insert the tip of the right-hand needle into the first stitch on the left-hand needle, going under the left-hand needle from front to back.

2. Set up the yarn in your right hand, as described on page 17, to work these stitches English style. Be sure to grab the yarn from the back of the work.

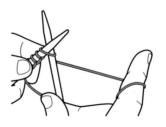

3. Holding the needles in your left hand in an X position, bring the yarn, attached to your right index finger, under the right-hand needle toward your left wrist and then back over the right-hand needle counterclockwise, wrapping the yarn around it.

4. Slowly inch the needle out of the stitch, until you are able to pull the "new" stitch out of the "old" stitch. It may be helpful to keep your left index finger on the stitch you're in, to keep it straight while you pull the right-hand needle out—and to use your right index finger to keep the "new" stitch taut.

5. Now slip off the left-hand needle the stitch you were just in, and restart the process from step 1.

Purling

The main difference between the knit and purl stitches is that the path of the needle is the exact opposite; instead of inserting the needle from front to back (as in the knit stitch), the needle moves from back to front.

1. Insert the tip of the right-hand needle into the first stitch on the left-hand needle, from back to front.

2. Set up the yarn in your right hand, as you did for working the knit stitch English style—being sure to grab the yarn from the front of the work.

3. Holding the needles in your left hand in an X position, bring the yarn, attached to your right index finger, over and then under the right-hand needle, wrapping the yarn around the needle counterclockwise.

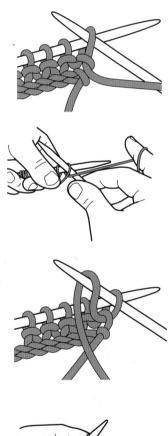

4. Slowly inch the needle out of the stitch, until you are able to push the "new" stitch out of the "old" stitch. It may be helpful to keep your left index finger on the stitch you're in, to help keep it straight while you pull the right-hand needle out— and to use your right index finger to keep the "new" stitch taut.

5. Now slip off the left-hand needle the stitch you were just in, and restart the process from step 1.

When you finish a row, switch the needles in your hands, and begin a row of knit or purl from step 1. Make sure the yarn is resting on the front of the work, and be careful not to make a stitch in the loose loop hanging below the first stitch.

Holding the yarn Continental style

If you've ever crocheted—or you're left-handed— Continental style may be just what you need! Many people find it a bit faster than English style, and easier on the wrists.

Knitting

To begin knitting Continental style, first cast on a few stitches using either the long-tail cast-on or cable cast-on method (see pages 14 and 16).

1. Set up the yarn in your left hand, as described on page 17, to work these stitches Continental style—be sure to grab the yarn from the back of the work.

2. Insert the tip of the right-hand needle into the first stitch on the left-hand needle, going under the left-hand needle from front to back.

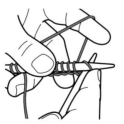

3. Without changing the setup of your hands, dip the right-hand needle so that it goes away from you and then under the yarn and toward you. This motion is called "picking" the yarn.

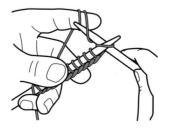

4. Place your right-hand index finger on top of the yarn wrapped around the right-hand needle. As you slide the right-hand needle out of the stitch, slide your index finger down to hold both the wrapped yarn and half of the stitch you're in, until the yarn comes out of the stitch.

5. Now slip off the left-hand needle the stitch you were just in, and restart the process from step 2.

Purling

As with English style, the main difference between the knit and purl stitches is that the path of the needle is the exact opposite; instead of inserting the needle from front to back (as in the knit stitch), the needle moves from back to front.

1. Set up the yarn in your left hand, as you did for working the knit stitch Continental style—be sure to grab the yarn from the front side of the work. Insert the tip of the right-hand needle into the first stitch on the left-hand needle, from back to front.

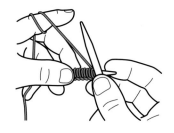

2. With the left index finger extended as for the knit stitch, pivot the right-hand needle so that it goes behind the yarn and picks it up. It may be helpful to drop your left index finger below the left-hand needle to help wrap the yarn all the way around the needle.

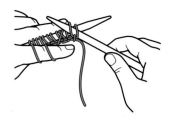

3. Once the yarn is fully wrapped around the needle, the right hand should catch the working yarn between the thumb and middle finger. Holding onto the yarn this way, ease the right-hand needle out of the stitch.

4. Now slip off the left-hand needle the stitch you were just in, and restart the process from step 1.

When you finish a row, switch the needles in your hands, and begin a row of knit or purl from step 1. Make sure the yarn is resting on the front of the work, and be careful not to make a stitch in the loose loop hanging below the first stitch.

Binding off

Binding off (also known as casting off) is the process of taking your stitches off the needles and securing them in place. Once bound off (if done correctly), the edge will never unravel.

1. Using whichever style of holding the yarn is most comfortable to you, knit two stitches.

2. Insert the tip of the left-hand needle into the first stitch you just knit—the stitch farthest from the tip of the right-hand needle—and, using your right index finger to hold the second stitch in place, pass the first stitch over the second stitch.

3. Bringing the second stitch over the first, drop this stitch off both needles—so that it ends up resting on the fabric between the tips of the two needles.

4. Once the stitch is bound off, knit another stitch and begin the process from step 2. Remember, you must have two stitches on the right-hand needle in order to cast off one stitch.

 Tip

Binding off isn't specific to the knit stitch. Try binding off in purl by purling two stitches onto the right-hand needle, and then slipping one over the other using the steps below. Similarly, try binding off in rib using the same technique.

5. When all the stitches have been cast off and one stitch remains, cut the yarn from the ball, leaving an eight-inch tail. Thread the tail through the remaining stitch on the needle, slip the stitch off the needle, and pull the tail to knot the last stitch. It's important you bind off loosely, otherwise the edge of the cast-off row will curve inward.

Reading a pattern

Reading a pattern is easy, once you know what you're looking at. Read it through a few times and mark anything you need to note, then take questions to your local knitting store or men's knitting group.

Finished measurements The smallest size is listed first; larger sizes are included in parentheses. The same method of listing the number of cast-on stitches, decreases, and so on, is repeated throughout the pattern, so it's a good idea to circle or underline the stitch counts that are relevant to your size when you first pick up the pattern.

Yarn What you'll need to make the model that the guy in the picture is wearing. It's OK to substitute different yarns, just be sure that you're getting the same number of stitches to the inch with your new yarn (see Gauge).

Needles The needle size you should use to get the required number of stitches per inch.

Notions Any extra materials that you'll need to complete the project.

Gauge An important measurement: if you get the suggested number of stitches and rows per inch, the garment will fit as it should.

Before starting a pattern, it's essential to make a gauge swatch in the stitches suggested to ensure proper fit. For more information on gauge, check out page 25.

Stitch patterns The stitches used in a pattern. If you're not familiar with the stitches, it's a good idea to test them out before starting the pattern.

Charts In some patterns, a chart will appear as a series of boxes (where each box equals one stitch) and will have its own set of symbols.

Schematics Many patterns include a schematic noting the important measurements of each garment. As described above under "Finished measurements," compare the size that you're making with the placement of the measurement within the parentheses.

Pattern abbreviations Most patterns include a list of abbreviations used in the pattern in case the pattern language doesn't make sense at first glance.

A few tips for beginners

Tips for left-handers Learning to knit as a left-hander can be challenging because the pictures in most books are designed for right-handed knitters. Remember that the needles should be switched in every situation. When a pattern says "put the needle with the stitches in your left hand and the empty needle in your right," you should do the exact opposite: the empty needle always goes in your left hand—this is the needle that does the "work." Next, remember that the direction of the yarn is the opposite in each situation. In right-handed knitting, the yarn is wrapped around the needle counterclockwise. In left-handed knitting, the yarn should always be wrapped clockwise.

If you're still having trouble learning to knit, find someone who knits right-handed, sit across the table from them, and watch how the needles move.

RS/WS In patterns you'll often see the abbreviations "RS" and "WS," which stand for "right side" and "wrong side." By knitting definition, the right side is the side that faces out when the garment is worn. A good way to mark the RS of the piece is to stick a safety pin in the fabric on the right side to remind you which side is which.

Recognizing your stitches Recognizing what a knit stitch looks like compared with a purl stitch becomes really important when you go to count your stitches. On the right side of stockinette stitch, a knit stitch looks like a V. On the wrong side of stockinette stitch, the purl stitch looks like a horizontal bump.

Stitch definition It's important to know what the stitches look like on the needle. Every stitch has two loops or "legs"—one loop comes down the front of the needle and the other down the back. Usually, on the left-hand needle, the loop on the side that's facing you should be leaning toward the tip of the left-hand needle. The loop on the back side should be leaning toward the back of the needle—away from the tip. The easiest way to determine whether a stitch is facing in the right direction is to pinch it with your fingers and flatten it out. If you've got the reverse, you're probably wrapping the yarn in the wrong direction. For each stitch that's twisted, slip it to the right-hand needle through the back loop of the stitch. Then insert the tip of the left-hand needle into the front of the stitch and slip it back to the left needle. This action will return the stitch to its correct position.

Gauge

Gauge is defined as the number of stitches and the number of rows you must work for each inch of knitted fabric. At the beginning of most patterns, a gauge requirement is given which implies that when the suggested needle size and yarn are used, the finished garment will fit the way that it was intended. Thus, before you start any pattern, it's very important to do a gauge swatch.

When examining yarn labels, you'll notice that a gauge measurement is represented by a grid with a set of numbers surrounding it (see page 12). Along the bottom and left-hand edges, you'll see the measurements 10 cm/4", indicating that the gauge of this yarn is measured over a 4" x 4" square. Along the top edge, you'll see a set of numbers which represents the number of stitches equaling 4". Along the right-hand edge, you'll see another set of numbers, representing the number of rows equaling 4". So, a yarn with 18 sts across the top edge and 20 across the right edge equals a yarn yielding a gauge of 4.5 sts per inch and 5 rows per inch.

Using the information on the yarn label, in conjunction with the gauge information in the pattern, make a swatch by casting on 20 stitches, and working Stockinette Stitch (a row of knit, a row of purl) for 26 rows. After you've bound off, measure your gauge by counting the number of stitches on the Right Side of the work that equal 1". When counting, don't be afraid to count half—or even quarter stitches; the more accurate your count, the better you are equipped to ensure proper fit.

In your gauge swatch, if the numbers match what the pattern suggests, you're in the clear. If they don't, you'll need to make a new gauge swatch, and adjust the needle size to get the appropriate gauge. To increase the number of stitches per inch, decrease the needle size (i.e. make the stitches smaller). To decrease the number of stitches per inch, increase the needle size (i.e. make the stitches larger).

Increasing

An increase shapes a garment by adding stitches per row, thus increasing the amount of fabric. In a Knit Front Back (Kfb), you knit first into the front of the stitch, and then into the back of the stitch, making two stitches from one. In an English Make 1 (M1), the bar between two stitches is picked up and twisted to create an extra stitch.

Knit Front Back (Kfb)

1. Insert the right-hand needle into the stitch in the same way as usual, wrap the yarn around the needle and remove it from the stitch, but do not slip the stitch off the needle. Pivot the right-hand needle like a scissor so that the tip now goes into the back loop of the stitch, right to left. Wrap the yarn around the needle and pull it out. Then slip the stitch off the left-hand needle, resulting in two new stitches on the right-hand needle.

English Make 1 (M1)

1. Knit the first stitch of the row as usual. Then, pulling the two needles apart slightly, insert the tip of the right-hand needle under the bar between the two stitches from front to back. Place the stitch on the left-hand needle by inserting the left needle into the back loop to slide it over. It should look twisted.

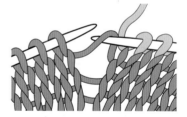

2. Knit into the front loop of the picked-up bar in the same way you would normally knit into a stitch. Note: This stitch may be a little tight and will take some easing to work.

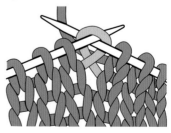

Decreasing

A decrease shapes garments by subtracting the number of stitches from a row, offering less fabric as a result. In a Knit 2 Together or a Purl 2 Together decrease, two stitches are knit or purled together to create a right-leaning decrease. In a Slip Slip Knit decrease, two stitches are slipped knitwise and then knit through the back loops to create a left-leaning decrease.

Knit 2 Together/Purl 2 Together (K2tog/P2tog)

1. When knitting or purling two stitches together, instead of inserting the tip of the right-hand needle into the first stitch, insert it into the first and second stitches. Wrap the yarn around the needle, pull the wrapped needle out of the stitch, and slip both stitches off the needle together.

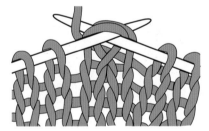

Slip Slip Knit (SSK)

1. Insert the tip of the right-hand needle as if to knit the next stitch, but instead of knitting it, just slip it from the left-hand needle to the right-hand needle. Repeat this step once more in the next stitch—there should now be two stitches that have been slipped knitwise on your right-hand needle.

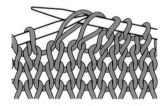

2. Insert the tip of the left-hand needle into the front loops of the two slipped stitches on the right-hand needle. Wrap the yarn around the right-hand needle, pull the yarn out of both stitches, and slip them off the left-hand needle together.

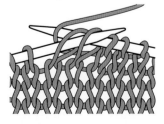

How to pick up stitches

Often, in knitted garments, bound-off or selvedge stitches are picked up to expand the form of a piece or to change the direction of the knitting. In sweaters, stitches are sometimes picked up around the armhole so that the sleeve can be worked. In socks, stitches up both sides of the heel flap are worked to join the heel to the foot; in the case of the Medallion Mitts, stitches are picked up in order to reduce holes at the thumb.

> **Tip**
>
> When picking up stitches, space out the number you need to pick up evenly along the edge to give a uniform look: usually 3 stitches for every 4 rows.

1. Examine the edge of the fabric you will be picking up—look for selvedge stitches, a bind-off or cast-on edge, knit or purl stitches—any space along an edge where you can insert a needle.

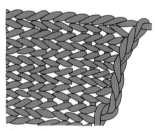

2. With the RS of the fabric facing you and moving from the front to the back, insert your needle under the two loops closest to the edge—in the example shown below, under two loops from a knit stitch.

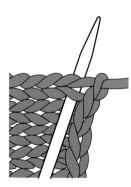

3. Holding the needle in the stitch in your left hand and the working needle in your right, knit the two loops together by inserting the working needle through the front loops of the stitches, then wrap the yarn around the needle and pull the loop out of the stitch.

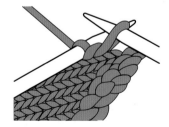

4. Slide the two loops off together, just as if you were knitting two stitches together. Insert your left-hand needle into the next stitch to be picked up, working across the fabric from right to left.

Accessories

Knit Wallet & Business Card Holder

In the corporate world, nothing says "professional man" like the classic, black leather wallet and silver business-card holder. But aren't there days when you're just ready to break free, stick it to the man, and be a little different? Here's your chance! The best of both worlds, this wallet and card holder will stand up to everyday use—and still look good during those stuffy business meetings and "optional" formal dinners.

Stitch Guide

Linen stitch

(Multiples of 2 plus 3)

Row 1: (RS) K1 *Sl 1 pwise wyif K1 repeat from * to end.

Row 2: P2 *Sl 1 pwise wyib P1 repeat from * to end P1.

Repeat rows 1 and 2 for patt.

below Unique, practical, and stylish accessories.

Knit Wallet

Finished measurements: 8.75" x 3.5", unfolded **Yarn:** Berroco Suede (120 yd.; 100% nylon; shade: Wild Bill Hickock, 3717; 1 ball **Needles:** US size-7 straight needles **Notions:** Tapestry needle

Gauge: 16 sts and 28 rows = 4" in St st; 20 sts and 32 rows = 4" in linen st

To save time and sanity:

TAKE TIME TO CHECK THE GAUGE.

Billfold

CO 41 sts. Knit 1 row. Beg with row 1 of linen stitch, work in patt for 3.5", ending on a WS row. Purl 4 rows. Beg on WS row, cont in patt stitch for another 3.5", ending on a WS row. Knit 1 row and BO all sts.

Pockets

Large pockets (make 2)

CO 17 sts. Knit 1 row. Beg with row 1 of linen stitch, work in patt for 2.5", ending on a WS row. Knit 1 row and BO all sts. Make a second pocket to match.

Medium pocket (make 1)

CO 21 sts. Knit 1 row. Beg with row 1 of linen stitch, work in patt for 2", ending on a WS row. Knit 1 row and BO all sts.

Finishing

Weave in the ends. Fold the billfold in half at purl rows. Whipstitch (see page 124) the seam on the left side and then the right side of the billfold to form the main part of the wallet. Place one large pocket on the seamed billfold, lining the left edge and bottom edges of the pocket with the left and bottom edges of the billfold. Whipstitch the pocket in place, sewing across the top, left, and bottom sides of the pocket; the right-hand edge of the pocket should remain unsewn. Repeat the process with the other large pocket, sewing it to the right-hand side of the billfold and leaving the left-hand edge of the large pocket unsewn.

Place the medium pocket on top of the large pocket on the right-hand side of the wallet and sew in place, leaving the top edge of this pocket unsewn.

Blocking

To flatten, place the dry closed wallet on a flat surface under several heavy books overnight. Do not wet.

Business Card Holder

Finished measurements: 2.25" x 3.75"

Yarn: Berroco Suede (120 yd.); 100% nylon; shade: Wild Bill Hickock, 3717; 1 ball

Needles: US size-7 straight needles

Notions: Tapestry needle **Gauge:** 16 sts and 28 rows = 4" in St st; 20 sts and 32 rows = 4" in linen st

To save time and sanity:

TAKE TIME TO CHECK THE GAUGE.

> **Tip**
>
> Linen stitch makes a firm, secure fabric—perfect for items like wallets and placemats. But when working the stitch pattern, be careful not to knit your stitches too tightly or it will be difficult to work them on the next row.

Pattern

CO 19 stitches. Knit 1 row. Work linen stitch, beg with row 1 of pattern, for 1", ending on a RS row. Purl 1 row. Beg on RS row, work linen stitch until piece measures 3.25" from start, ending on a RS row. Purl 1 row. Beg on RS row, work linen stitch for 2.25", ending on a WS row. Piece should measure 5.5" from start. Knit 1 row and BO all sts.

Finishing

Weave in the ends. Fold the holder in half so that the two sections that measure 2.25" rest on top of one another. Whipstitch side seams together.

Blocking

To flatten the cardholder, place on a flat surface under several heavy books overnight. Do not wet.

Felted Military Belt

During both World Wars in the twentieth century, people banded together to knit for the troops. Little did they know that the troops were on the other side of the sea knitting for themselves. Besides being a fulfilling way to spend downtime, knitting provided an immediate source of much-needed socks, gloves, hats, and more. In true homage to this soldierly history, the Felted Military Belt can withstand almost any force. Knitted quickly on big needles, the belt is felted after you've bound off, giving it both strength and stability.

Stitch Guide

Seed stitch

(Multiples of 2)

Row 1: *K1 P1* repeat from *.

Row 2: *P1 K1* repeat from *.

Repeat rows 1 and 2 for patt.

below Mix and match your colors to suit your wardrobe.

Finished measurements: 48" x 1" (Note: The length may vary depending on how aggressively the belt is felted.) **Yarn:** Noro Kureyon (109 yd.); 100% wool; shades: 52 and 170; 1 ball of each (will make several belts) **Needles:** US size-11 straight needles **Notions:** Tapestry needle; fabric glue; 2 x 1.5" D-rings; embroidery thread **Gauge (pre-felt):** 12 sts and 19 rows = 4" in St st

To save time and sanity:

TAKE TIME TO CHECK THE GAUGE.

Version 1

CO 8 sts. Work seed stitch patt for 62".
BO all sts and weave in the ends.

Version 2 (for a stiffer belt)

CO 8 sts. Holding two strands together
(one from each end of the ball), work garter
stitch (knit every stitch) until piece measures
62". BO all sts.

> ### Tip
> Your local hardware store has all kinds of
> knitting goodies that you won't necessarily
> find at a yarn store: D-rings for this belt,
> for example—along with a whole host of
> other items, such as rubber washers,
> which can double as stitch markers.

Finishing

Felt the belt in your washing machine according
to the instructions given on page 37. When
completely felted, hold the belt at both ends
and give it a nice tug to stretch out the fibers
and increase the length. Allow the belt to dry
overnight by hanging it over a door knob or shower
rod. When completely dry, place both D-rings
on top of one another and slide them onto the
belt, with the flat edge resting inside the fabric,
approximately 3" from the end of the belt. Outline
the fabric between the D-rings and the edge of
the fabric with fabric glue, making sure to run a
line of glue on both sides of the D-rings. Fold the
glued side of the belt over the D-rings and press
down firmly. Let the belt dry overnight.

When it is dry, scrape off any glue that made
its way through the fabric. Using a needle and
some embroidery thread, stitch through the
fabric and around the two D-rings to secure
them in place. If desired, secure the fabric folded
over the rings using the same technique.

How to felt

Felting is the process of (intentionally) dropping a garment made of wool (or another feltable fiber, such as alpaca or mohair) into hot water and then agitating it—causing the fibers to lock together tightly.

The easiest way to get a good, strong felted fabric is to find a top-loading washing machine with an adjustable dial. Start your washing machine on its lowest water-level setting, its heaviest agitation cycle, and its hottest water temperature. Drop in a tablespoon or two of natural liquid soap (stay away from commercial laundry soaps, which may cause the dye in your yarn to run), and let the barrel fill with water. Enclose the items to be felted in a zippered laundry bag—or even a pillowcase with a rubber band at the top. (This is important: during the felting process, little bits of wool will shed from your garment and may cause your washing machine's filter to jam if the garments are not in a bag of some sort.)

When the machine begins to agitate, drop the bag filled with items to be felted into the washing machine and let the cycle run for about 10 minutes. Then open the lid and check on your garments. If the stitches still look loose, put the garment back in the bag and let it go for another 5 minutes—be sure to turn the agitation dial back, if necessary.

> **Tip**
>
> When weaving in ends on an item that's going to be felted, be especially careful that the ends aren't knotted tightly or woven too thickly in a single place. Too much extra yarn in one place can leave an unsightly bulge in the finished fabric.

Continue checking on the status of your garments every 5 minutes or so. Some yarns and garments felt more quickly than others, so it's important to keep a watchful eye on them. When the fibers are fuzzy and locked, the fabric is stiff, and it's difficult to distinguish your stitches from one another, it's done. Be sure to check the finished felted measurements of the item as it starts to look done. Items can be felted again and again—even after they've dried—but you can't "unfelt" something if it gets too small!

Remove the bag from the machine before the rinse cycle. Plunge the felted items into cold water, then roll them up in a towel to soak up any remaining water. Allow them to dry as indicated by the pattern—be sure to take advantage of the drying process to block your items.

Fisherman's Watchcap & Scarf Set

Historically, watchcaps were knit for (and by) fishermen using a lanolin-rich worsted-weight wool. The combination of tight stitches and a snug cuff doubled over the ears provided an impenetrable barrier against wind and salt from the sea. Today, every guy (fisherman or not) needs a warm hat to face the elements. This classic watchcap and ribbed scarf set is made from Cascade Pastaza's combination of llama and wool, designed especially to provide warmth. The fisherman's rib gives way to a long-lasting elasticity, providing multiple layers to keep any guy warm on a blustery day.

Stitch Guide

Fisherman's rib A

(worked in the rnd)

(Multiples of 2)

Rnd 1: *P1 K1 in st below repeat from *.

Rnd 2: *P1 K1 repeat from *.

Repeat rnds 1 and 2 for patt.

below Durable protection against the elements.

Fisherman's Watchcap

Finished measurements: 11" tall, 21" circumference (relaxed) **Yarn:** Cascade Pastaza (132 yd.); 50% llama, 50% wool; shade 070; 2 skeins **Needles:** 16", US size-8 circular needle; set of US size-8 double-pointed needles

Notions: Tapestry needle; stitch marker

Gauge: 16 sts and 22 rows = 4" in St st

To save time and sanity:

TAKE TIME TO CHECK THE GAUGE.

Pattern

With the circular needle, CO 72 stitches using the long-tail method (see page 14). Join, being careful not to twist the stitches, and place marker (PM). Knit 1 row. Beg with row 1 of fisherman's rib A, working in patt until piece measures 4". **Next rnd:** Begin St st and work until piece measures 8" from CO.

Shape top: Decrease for top of hat as follows, switching to double-pointed needles when the number of stitches becomes too few to work comfortably.

Rnd 1: *K7 K2tog repeat from * 8 times (64 sts).
Rnd 2 (and every remaining even-numbered rnd): Knit.
Rnd 3: *K6 K2tog repeat from * 8 times (56 sts).
Rnd 5: *K5 K2tog repeat from * 8 times (48 sts).
Rnd 7: *K4 K2tog repeat from * 8 times (40 sts).
Rnd 9: *K3 K2tog repeat from * 8 times (32 sts).
Rnd 11: *K2 K2tog repeat from * 8 times (24 sts).
Rnd 13: *K1 K2tog repeat from * 8 times (16 sts).
Rnd 15: *K2tog repeat from * 8 times (8 sts).
Rnd 17: *K2tog repeat from * 4 times (4 sts).

Finishing

Break the yarn, leaving a 10" tail. With the tail threaded onto a tapestry needle, remove your marker, draw the needle through the remaining stitches, and close the top by pulling the yarn tightly. Weave in the ends.

> **Tip**
>
> To work stockinette stitch in the round, remember there are no purls. By knitting every stitch in the round, you get the same fabric if you were to knit back and forth, knitting one row, then purling the next.

Fisherman's Scarf

Finished measurements: 60" long x 7.5" wide **Yarn:** Cascade Pastaza (132 yd.); 50% llama, 50% wool; shade 070; 3 skeins **Needles:** 16", US size-8 circular needle or US size 8 straight needles **Notions:** Tapestry needle **Gauge:** 16 sts and 22 rows = 4" in St st

To save time and sanity:

TAKE TIME TO CHECK THE GAUGE.

Pattern

CO 31 sts. Beg with row 1 of Fisherman's rib B, work in patt until piece measures 60", ending on a WS row. BO all sts loosely. Weave in the ends.

Stitch Guide

Fisherman's rib B

(worked back and forth)

(Multiples of 2 plus 3)

Row 1: (RS) K1 *K1 P1 repeat from * to end K2.

Row 2: K1 *P1 K1 repeat from *.

Row 3: K1 *K1 in st below, P1 repeat from * to end K1 in st below, K1.

Repeat rows 2 and 3 for patt.

Fisherman's rib

Though it looks like a standard 1 x 1 rib, the fisherman's rib makes a deep, lofty ribbing that creates a double layer of fabric, making it ideal for hats and scarves. Knitting into the stitch in the row below is simple: look for the V-shaped opening just below the stitches on the needle and insert the needle in your right hand here.

1. Work set-up row as described in patt st. On the next row, purl the first stitch. Then insert the right-hand needle into the V-shaped opening at the base of the stitch on the left-hand needle.

2. Once inside the stitch, wrap the yarn around the needle and pull from the stitch, sliding it off the left-hand needle.

3. Continue in pattern, spacing a purl stitch in between each stitch worked in the row below (as described in Step 2), through the end of the row, following the patt st.

Tip

For complex stitch patterns where you think you might have trouble ripping back and picking up the stitches, try inserting a rip cord every few rows by putting some dental floss on a tapestry needle and threading it through each stitch. If you end up ripping back, the rip cord will hold your stitches and prevent them from unraveling while you pick them up.

Working on double points

To create any seamless garment, you need to work in the round! In the case of the Fisherman's watchcap, you'll work with double-pointed needles when the crown of the cap gets too small to work on the circular needle—giving you the chance to work out the technique before starting to work with them from the beginning of a garment.

1. Begin by casting on all stitches onto one double-pointed needle. Note: It's okay if the stitches bunch up on this needle.

2. When all stitches have been cast on, carefully slip each stitch purlwise onto the other double-pointed needles in the set, dividing the stitches evenly among the set, and saving one to use as the working needle. For example, 60 stitches evenly distributed over 3 double-pointed needles means that each needle would hold 20 stitches (20 x 3 = 60); the fourth needle of the set would be empty.

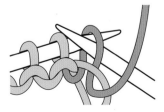

3. Next, arrange the three needles so that they form a triangle. Hold the needle with the slip knot in your left hand, and the needle with the working yarn in your right, being careful to keep the triangle balanced.

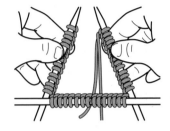

4. Insert a new double-pointed needle into the slip knot and knit it. Then, begin working across the first double-pointed needle, in pattern.

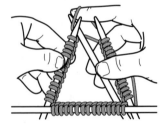

5. When you reach the end, you will notice that the needle that was holding these first stitches is now empty. Turning the work clockwise, and now using the empty needle, begin working the stitches on the next needle. Repeat this process every time you empty a needle.

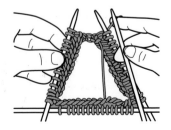

Multi-Media Cozy

Mobile digital devices get abused—in fact they're built to resist accidental drops. Still, they can only hit the pavement so many times before some serious damage is done. The Multi-Media Cozy is knit in Ultramerino 6, a merino wool that provides a healthy dose of extra protection, without bulking out your pockets with lots of extra fabric. This pattern is sized for various types of iPod® mobile digital devices*.

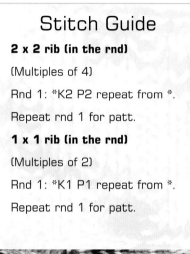

Stitch Guide

2 x 2 rib (in the rnd)

(Multiples of 4)

Rnd 1: *K2 P2 repeat from *.

Repeat rnd 1 for patt.

1 x 1 rib (in the rnd)

(Multiples of 2)

Rnd 1: *K1 P1 repeat from *.

Repeat rnd 1 for patt.

below Smart guys keep their multi-media players safe.

To fit iPod® mobile digital devices with the following dimensions: 3.5" x 1.5" (3.75" x 2", 4" x 2.5") **Yarn:** Artyarns Ultramerino 6 100g (274 yd.); 100% luxury merino wool; shade 117; 1 skein will make several cozies **Needles:** Set of 5 US size-3 double-pointed needles **Notions:** Tapestry needle; stitch marker **Gauge:** 24 sts and 32 rows = 4" in St st

To save time and sanity:

TAKE TIME TO CHECK THE GAUGE.

* This pattern has not been authorized, sponsored, or otherwise approved by Apple Computer, Inc. iPod is a trademark of Apple Computer, Inc.

Version 1

Cast on 20 (28, 32) sts.
Divide sts evenly across
3 dpns and join for working
in the rnd, being careful not
to twist the sts, and place
marker (PM). Begin 1 x 1 rib and work in patt
until piece measures 2".

Next rnd: Begin 2 x 2 rib patt and work until
piece measures 5" (5.5", 6") from CO.

Finishing

Divide sts so that half rest on one dpn and
the other half on a second dpn. BO sts using a
three-needle bindoff (see page 121) and weave
in the ends.

Version 2

Cast on 6 sts onto 4 dpns.
Distribute sts as foll: 2 sts
are on needle 1, 1 st is on
needle 2, 2 sts are on needle
3, and 1 st is on needle 4.
Join for working in the rnd.

Knit 1 rnd, placing marker between last two sts
to mark beg of rnd. Beg increases as foll:

Rnd 1: Kfb into every st (12 sts).

Rnd 2: * Kfb K2 Kfb Kfb K1 repeat from * once
(18 sts).

Rnd 3: *KFb K4, Kfb K3 repeat from * (22 sts).
Cont increasing as set, increasing at beg of
every needle and at end of needles 1 and 3
every even rnd (6 sts increased) and at beg
and end of needles 1 and 3 only, every odd rnd
(4 sts increased) until 6 (8, 10) rnd in total
have been worked: 48 (52, 62) sts. Work two
rnd even, without increases.

Next rnd: Place buttonhole for earphone plug
as foll: for upper right placement, knit to 5
before end of needle 1; for upper (or lower)
center placement, K3 sts on needle 1; for
lower left placement, K1 on needle 3; double
yarn over, K2tog knit to end of rnd, dropping
the second yarn over off the needle on the
next rnd. Work 4 (5, 7) rnds straight.

Next rnd: *K4 K2tog repeat from * to end, K0
(K4, K2). BO all sts loosely. Weave in the ends.

To use: remove headphones from player. Then
stretch the cover across the back, leaving the
face of the player open. Arrange the cozy so
that the buttonhole rests at the plug for the
headphones, and reinsert the plug.

Ribbing

Ribbing combines the knit and purl stitches in the same row to create an elastic fabric, and is often used in garments to secure the fabric to the body. In socks and gloves, for example, ribbing is used on the leg and wrist to keep the item from falling down. Here's how to knit ribbing, using a 2 x 2 (K2 P2) rib as an example:

Tip

The secret to ribbing is to always remember to "knit the knits" and "purl the purls" as they face you, on the row you're working on.

1. Knit the first two stitches on the left-hand needle. Bring the yarn in between the tips of the needles to the front of the work.

2. With the yarn on the front of the work, purl the next two stitches. Bring the yarn in between the tips of the needles to the back of the work.

3. Begin the process from step 1, working to the end of the row and always bringing the yarn between the tips of the needles, to the front or back of the work. After a few rows your work should look like this. Note the "columns" of similar stitches moving upward.

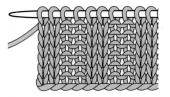

Camo Coffee-Cup Cozy

You know those cardboard sleeves you pick up with your latte on the way to work in the morning? Next time, save a tree and take your Camo Coffee-Cup Cozy instead. A great opportunity to practice Fair Isle in the round, the cozy takes advantage of the double layer of fabric created by this technique to prevent your fingers from getting too hot while holding your beverage. And lest a cozy seem too feminine, the camouflage injects a heavy dose of masculinity.

Stitch Guide

3 x 4 rib A (in the rnd)

(Multiples of 7)

Row 1: *K4 P3 repeat from *.

Repeat row 1 for patt.

below Take a break without getting your fingers burned!

Finished measurements: 10" circumference at widest point x 4" tall **Yarn:** Dalegarn Heilo 50g (110 yd.); 100% wool: shade: 3841, 1 ball (MC); shade: 8972, 1 ball (CC) **Needles:** Set of 4 US size-3 double-pointed needles **Notions:** Tapestry needle; stitch marker **Gauge:** 28 sts and 28 rows = 4" in camouflage chart using St st

To save time and sanity:

TAKE TIME TO CHECK THE GAUGE.

Pattern

With MC, CO 63 sts. Divide sts evenly among three double-pointed needles: 21 sts on each needle. Join for working in the rnds, being careful not to twist sts. PM. Work in 4 x 3 rib for 4 rnds; then begin row 1 of camouflage chart. Work 10 rnds as charted.

Next rnd: At beg and end of each needle, dec 1 st (6 sts decreased), working rem rnds as charted.

Next rnd: With MC, dec 1 st at beg and end of each needle. BO all sts. Weave in the ends.

Tip

Keeping your place in a chart can be difficult if the chart is large or complex. Try using a card or a sticky note to mark the row you're working, and move it up (or down) after each complete row.

Camouflage chart

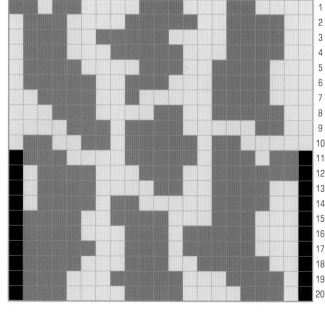

1
2
3
4
5
6
7
8
9
10
11
12
13
14
15
16
17
18
19
20

Note: Chart is worked from right to left in the rnd, and from top to bottom

Finishing

Wet the cozy thoroughly with cold water, then roll in a towel to remove any remaining moisture. Turning a large paper coffee cup upside down, place the cozy over the cup at the greatest width and allow to dry overnight.

CC

MC

No Stitch

Fair Isle knitting

Also known as "stranded knitting," Fair Isle knitting is one of the two primary methods of adding more than one color in the same row. In Fair Isle knitting (versus intarsia, see page 96) the yarns are carried behind the work across the entire garment. Once complete, the wrong side of the fabric shows the "floats," or strands of yarn.

Holding the yarn in both hands

Traditionally Fair Isle worked in the round is done by holding two different colors (one in each hand) and carrying them along the back of the work throughout the piece. This technique—though difficult to master at first—makes Fair Isle knitting both easy and fast. Before trying to hold yarn in both your right and left hands at the same time and working with them, try practicing a few rows (or even a whole scarf) holding it in the hand you don't normally use to knit with. If you've always knit Continental style, try English style for a while. Know nothing but holding the yarn in your right hand? Try holding it in your left hand and "picking" a bit! (See page 20 for help.)

Knitting Fair Isle

Once you've practiced the style you're not used to, you're ready to try working with two different colors: one in each hand.

1. Once your stitches are cast on, knit the first two stitches with color A.

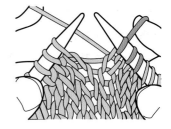

2. Then knit the next two stitches with color B.

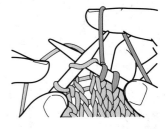

3. Keep alternating between the two hands as necessary, according to the chart. Once you've got the tension down, it's easy!

Aran Laptop Cover

Those days of sitting at home surfing the Net alone are long gone, so don't let your fear of taking your laptop out and about prevent you from finding undiscovered hot spots! Slip on this laptop cover, toss it in your messenger bag, and you're set! Cabled fabric inherently provides extra cushion and security—which makes it perfect for protecting your priceless data and MP3 collection from the perils of the world beyond your doorstep.

> **Tip**
>
> Want to add a bit of extra stability or security to your cover? Try sewing in a layer of felt—or some craftboard interface—to the inside before finishing the piece. The extra fabric helps hold your laptop snug inside.

below Cabled meets wireless!

Finished measurements: 10" (11", 11") x 12"(14.5", 15.5") **Yarn:** Peace Fleece (200 yd.); 30% mohair, 70% wool; shade: Negotiation Gray; 3 skeins **Needles:** 24", US size-8 circular needle **Notions:** Tapestry needle; stitch markers; safety pins (3); 1" quick-release clips **Gauge:** 15 sts and 24 rows = 4" in St st

To save time and sanity:
TAKE TIME TO CHECK THE GAUGE.

Pattern

The first stitch of every row is slipped purlwise throughout. CO 64 (72, 76) sts.

Row 1: (WS) Sl 1 pwise, K1, P2 (4, 5), K2, place marker (PM), work first row of long rope cable right, PM, P2 (4, 5), PM, work first row of wild oak cable, PM, P2 (4, 5), PM, work first row of long rope cable left, PM, K2, P2 (4, 5), K2.

Row 2: Sl 1 pwise P1 K2 (4, 5) P2, work second row of long rope cable left, K2 (4, 5), work second row of wild oak cable, K2 (4, 5), work second row of long rope cable right, P2 K2 (4, 5) P1 K1.

Cont in patt as established and as charted until piece measures 10.5" (11.5", 11.5"), ending on a RS row. Mark on your charts where you've stopped for each. Do not remove markers.

Fold

Next row (WS): Knit.

Next row: Purl.

Cont in reverse St st for 2", ending on a purl row. Restart cable repeats, as established, beg from where you left off. Cont working as set until piece measures 27.5" (28.5", 28.5") from CO, ending on a WS row.

Flap

The top edge of the flap is bound off to form three panels, which will later be attached to the front edge of the cover.

BO first 18 (21, 23) sts, slip 1 pwise K1 (2, 2), cont working wild oak cable, K2 (3, 3). Start a new ball of yarn and BO the rem 18 (21, 23) sts. Break yarn and pull through at end of row.

Next row: On rem sts Sl 1 pwise P1 (2, 2), work next row of wild oak cable, P2 (3, 3). Cont as established for 1", ending on a WS row. BO rem sts and weave in the ends.

Finishing

Lay the cover on a flat surface with the WS facing up. Fold the bottom half of the cover up so that the fold rests 1" into the reverse stockinette section. Using safety pins, pin the two edges together on both sides to secure them for seaming.

With yarn threaded on a tapestry needle, starting at the top of the seams, whipstitch the edges together 1" before fold. Flatten the last inch of fabric to form a T-shape and whipstitch the flattened seam. Repeat on the other side. Turn the cover inside out so that the RS is visible. Sew the top portion of the clip to the top flap of the cover at the center of each of the panels. Slip the cover onto the laptop and fold the flap over. Pull the edge of the cover down across the laptop, stretching it slightly. With safety pins, mark the location of the lower portion of the clip for each clasp. Remove the laptop and sew the lower portion of the clips to the laptop cover.

Wild oak cable

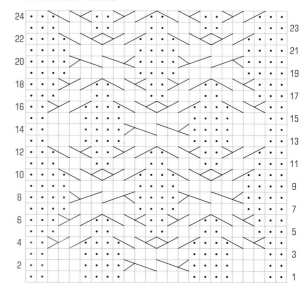

Long rope cable left

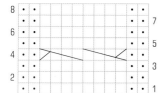

Long rope cable right

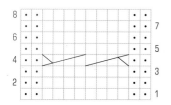

Note: RS rows are worked from right to left, WS rows are worked left to right.

☐   knit on a RS row, purl on a WS row

·   purl on a RS row, knit on a WS row

slip 4 sts to a cable needle and hold at front, K4, K4 from cable needle

slip 4 st to a cable needle and hold at back of work, K4, K4 from cable needle

slip 3 sts to a cable needle and hold at front, K3, K3 from cable needle

slip 3 sts to a cable needle and hold at back, K3, K3 from cable needle

slip 3 sts to a cable needle and hold at front of work, P1, K3 from cable needle

slip 1 st to a cable needle and hold at back of work, K3, P1 from cable needle

The knitted cable

Often resembling a rope or twist, a knitted cable is the process of switching the order of one or more groups of stitches. For example, in a grouping of four stitches, instead of knitting stitches 1 and 2 first, you skip them by placing them on a cable needle and working on stitches 3 and 4, before returning to work on 1 and 2. This process is illustrated below.

> **Tip**
>
> A short double-pointed needle is a great substitute if you can't find your cable needle, or your local yarn store is fresh out.

1. Slip the required number of stitches onto a cable needle by inserting the tip of the cable needle into the stitches on the left-hand needle one at a time as though to purl. In the illustration here, two stitches are being transferred to the cable needle.

2. Hold these stitches at the front (or back, depending on the pattern) of the work. Skipping over the held stitches momentarily, knit the next two stitches on the needle.

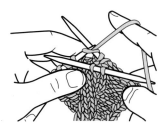

3. Now go back and knit the two stitches held on the cable needle. Note: These stitches may be a little tight until you get used to the technique—this is normal.

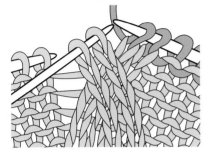

4. Continue working the rest of the row as indicated by the pattern.

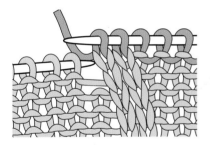

5. When working the next row of these cables, they may also appear a little tight, which is normal. In order to reduce holes between your cable and the neighboring stitches, give the yarn a little tug before and after working the cable stitches.

Chu'llu Hat and Scarf

The Chu'llu is a **South American Fair Isle** cap with deep earflaps. There, it's not unusual to see boys and men knitting their own Chu'llu. Inspired by the Chu'llu design, the pattern for the hat mixes a band of Fair Isle worked back and forth with an earflap that extends around the back of the head to create a snug-fitting winter cap.

Stitch Guide

2 x 2 rib (in the rnd)

(Multiples of 4)

Row 1: *K2 P2 repeat from *.

Repeat row 1 for patt.

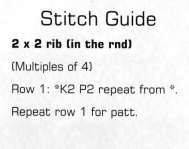

below This hat and scarf look great as a set or on their own.

Finished measurements: Scarf 7" wide x 60" long; hat 20" circumference (relaxed) **Yarn:** Brown Sheep Lamb's Pride Worsted (190 yd.); 85% wool, 15% mohair; shade: Old Sage M-69: 3 skeins (MC); Deep Charcoal M-06: 1 skein (CC1); Crème M-10: 1 skein (CC2); quantity is sufficient to make both projects **Needles:** Set of 4 US size-8 double-pointed needles; US size-8 straight needles; US size-7 straight needles (for hat only) **Notions:** Tapestry needle; stitch marker **Gauge:** 18 sts and 24 rows = 4" in St st on larger needles; 21 sts and 24 rows = 4" in St st using Chu'llu chart; 16 sts and 24 rows = 4" in diamond brocade

To save time and sanity:

TAKE TIME TO CHECK THE GAUGE.

Hat

With MC and US size-8 dpns, CO 8 sts. Divide sts evenly across dpns and join for working in the rnd, being careful not to twist sts. PM. Knit 1 rnd.

Next rnd: Kfb into every st (16 sts). Knit 1 rnd without increases.

Next rnd: *Kfb K1 repeat from * (24 sts). Knit 1 rnd without increases.

Next rnd: *Kfb K2 repeat from * (32 sts). Cont increasing every other rnd, adding one st to the count in bet increases, seven more times, switching to a 16" circular needle if necessary (88 sts). Work in St st until piece measures 6" from start.

Next rnd: Begin 2 x 2 rib and work for 1". From marker, BO next 32 sts and join CC2. Knit rem 56 sts. Purl 1 row.

Next row: Beg with row 9, work Chu'llu Chart, repeating pattern 7 times across row, through once.

Next row: (WS) Work 2 rows in St st, beg with a purl row. Rejoin MC and cont in St st until flap measures 5" from rib, ending on a WS row. Change to US size-7 needles and purl 2 rows. Beg with a knit row, cont in St st until work measures 5" from purl ridge. BO loosely and sew facing to back of flap. Weave in the ends.

Scarf

With CC2, CO 32 sts. Work 12 rows in garter st. Beg Chu'llu, chart working Fair Isle technique in St st, rep 4 times across row, and work rows 1–9 through once.

Next row: With CC2, inc 9 sts evenly across row. Purl 1 row. With MC, beg diamond brocade pattern and work until piece measures 55" from start, ending on a WS row.

Next row: With CC2, dec 9 sts evenly across row. Purl 1 row. Beg row 9 of Chu'llu chart, rep 4 times across row, and work rows 9–1 through once. With CC2, work 12 rows in garter st. BO all sts loosely. Weave in the ends.

Chu'llu Chart

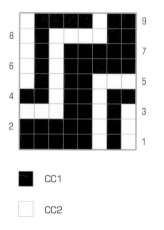

■ CC1

□ CC2

Note: RS rows are worked from right to left, WS rows from left to right

Stitch Guide

Diamond brocade

(Multiples of 8 plus 1)

Row 1: (RS) K4 *P1 K7 repeat from *, ending P1 K4.

Row 2: P3 *K1 P1 K1 P5 repeat from *, ending last repeat P3.

Row 3: K2 *P1 K3 repeat from *, ending last repeat K2.

Row 4: P1 *K1 P5 K1 P1 repeat from *.

Row 5: *P1 K7 repeat from *, ending P1.

Row 6: P1 *K1 P5 K1 P1 repeat from *.

Row 7: K2 *P1 K3 repeat from *, ending last repeat K2.

Row 8: P3 *K1 P1 K1 P5 repeat from *, ending last repeat P3.

Repeat rows 1–8 for patt.

> **Tip**
>
> If it's hard to distinguish the chart that you're reading, try taking it to a photocopier and having it enlarged.

Not-So-Rugged Scarf

Mohair on a man is practically unheard of, mainly because the fineness of the fiber is a bit too wispy for most men's tastes. Still, mohair is incredibly warm and soft against the neck, and in the right combination of colors and fibers, "girly" easily becomes "unique." The Not-So-Rugged Scarf mixes two luxurious yarns from Alchemy (both blended with silk) to create a muffler that is both warm and stylish.

> **Tip**
>
> Circular needles come in many lengths and sizes. When choosing a circular yarn for your project, be sure you've got the right length—or one that's within two or three inches of the one you need.

below The artistic look, knit on a circular needle.

Finished measurements: 67" circumference x 7.5" wide **Yarn:** Alchemy Yarns Haiku 25g (325 yd.); 40% silk, 60% mohair; shade: 65e Dragon (MC), 1 skein; Alchemy Yarns Synchronicity 50g (110 yd.); 50% silk, 50% merino wool; shade: 55c Montreat Path (CC), 1 skein

Needles: 24", US size-8 circular needle

Notions: Tapestry needle; stitch marker

Gauge: 14 sts x 26 rnds = 4" in St st

To save time and sanity:
TAKE TIME TO CHECK THE GAUGE.

Pattern

With CC, CO 240 sts. Join for working in the
rnd, being careful not to twist stitches. PM.
Knit 1 rnd. Cut yarn. Beg body of scarf and
work as foll, cutting yarn at each color change:
6 rnds MC, 2 rnds CC, 36 rnds MC, 2 rnds CC,
6 rnds MC, 1 rnd CC. BO all sts loosely and
weave in the ends.

Finishing

Block, if desired, by gently wetting the scarf
with cool water, then pinning it down flat against
a bedspread or towel to the desired length.

Tip

To make your bound-off
edge look looser and more
relaxed, work with a needle
a few sizes larger than
what is called for in the
pattern when you bind off.

Working on circular needles

In order to create any seamless garment, you've got to learn to work in the round! Circular needles come in many lengths—and it's important to be sure the number of stitches in your pattern will fit comfortably around the length of your circular needle before you start.

1. Cast on the required number of stitches, allowing the stitches to slide onto and around the cable portion of the needle. When all the stitches have been cast on, be sure there are no twists in the cast-on row—the entire cast on edge should face inward.

2. To join the stitches for working in the round, hold the circular needle so that the needle tip with the first stitch rests in your left hand and the needle tip with the working yarn rests in your right hand.

3. Knit the first stitch by inserting the tip of the right-hand needle, wrapping the yarn around the needle and completing the stitch as you would normally.

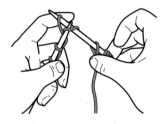

4. From this point on, knitting is no different than it would be if you were on straight needles—except that you don't have to purl to create stockinette stitch!

Hiking Boot Socks

Whether hiking up a steep hill or just pounding the pavement up those steps from the subway, every guy knows the difference that a pair of socks makes in determining how far he goes—and what shape his feet are in when he gets there. These Hiking Boot Socks use the bulkiness of Madil's Iceland yarn to produce just the right amount of support. What's more, this quick knit offers a great first attempt at knitting socks!

below Hand knit socks—great to sink your feet into.

Stitch Guide

3 x 2 rib (in the rnd)

(Multiples of 5)

Rnd 1: *K3 P2 repeat from *.

Repeat rnd 1 for patt.

Heel stitch

Row 1: *Sl 1 pwise K1 repeat from *.

Row 2: Sl 1 pwise purl.

Row 3: Sl 1 pwise K 2 *Sl 1 pwise K1 repeat from *, end K1.

Row 4: Sl 1 pwise purl.

Repeat rows 1–4 for patt.

Finished measurements: Cuff to heel: 11"; heel to toe: 10"; cuff circumference: 8.5" **Yarn:** Madil Iceland (137 yd.); 100% superwash wool; shade: 264, 2 balls (MC); shade 262, 1 ball (CC) **Needles:** Set of 4 US size-8 double-pointed needles **Notions:** Tapestry needle; stitch marker **Gauge:** 16 sts and 23 rows = 4" in St st

To save time and sanity:

TAKE TIME TO CHECK THE GAUGE.

Cuff

With MC, CO 35 sts using the long-tail method (see page 14). Divide sts among 3 double-pointed needles as follows: 10 sts on the first, 15 sts on the second, and 10 sts on the third. Join for working in the rnd and PM. Knit 1 rnd.

Next row: Beg 3 x 2 rib pattern and work in patt for 2". Continuing to work in 3 x 2 rib, change colors according to the foll stripe sequence: 3 rnd CC, 3 rnd MC, 6 rnd CC, 3 rnd MC, 3 rnd CC. Change to MC and continue in patt until piece measures 6" from start. Change to St st and work even until piece measures 9" from start.

Heel flap

The heel flap (the fabric that comprises the back of the heel) is worked over slightly fewer than half of the total number of sock stitches. Here, these 16 sock stitches are worked on one double-pointed needle, while the remaining 19 stitches rest on the other two double-pointed needles until you're ready to work the instep.

Setup for heel flap

Working from the marker, K8 sts, sl rem 2 sts to second needle. Turn work. Sl 1 pwise, and P15 sts; use the same needle to work all 15. Sl rem 2 sts onto second needle. Sl 10 of the 19 sts on second needle onto one of the empty needles, and hold for instep. Working across these 16 sts only, beg heel stitch patt, rep rows 1–4 four times.

Heel turn

The heel turn is the fabric that pulls the edges of the heel flap inward. Through a sequence of short rows, the heel is shaped by knitting together two stitches that lie on either side of a visible "gap." The heel turn is worked back and forth on one needle as foll:

Row 1: K9 sl marker K2tog K1 turn.

Row 2: P2 sl marker P2tog P1 turn.

Row 3: K2 sl marker K2tog (knitting one stitch from either side of the gap together).

Row 4: P4 sl marker P2tog (purling one stitch from either side of the gap) P1 turn.

Repeat rows 3 and 4, continuing to K2tog or P2tog one stitch from either side of the gap and working one more stitch, then turning the work, until 1 st remains beyond the gap on either side. Work the final rows as foll:

Row 1: Knit to 1 before gap and K2tog turn.

Row 2: Purl to 1 before gap and P2tog (8 sts rem).

Gusset

To work the gusset, first pick up selvedge stitches from one side of the heel flap, then knit across the stitches held from the instep, and finally pick up selvedge stitches down the other side of the heel flap. Then, you will begin decreasing two stitches every other row, until you have the same number of stitches as you cast on for the cuff.

With your empty needle, work across the remaining heel stitches. With the same needle (needle 1), pick up and knit 9 sts up the left-hand side of the heel flap. With your empty needle (needle 2), knit across 19 instep stitches. Then, with an empty needle (needle 3), pick up and knit 9 sts down the right-hand side of the heel flap and work to 1 st before the marker (45 sts).

The stitches should be arranged among the three needles so that half of the remaining heel stitches and the stitches picked up from the left-hand side of the heel flap are on needle 1, the stitches from the instep are on needle 2, and half of the remaining heel stitches and the stitches picked up from the right-hand side of the heel flap are on needle 3.

Decrease for foot

Rnd 1: Starting at your marker, work to 3 sts before the end of needle 1, SSK K1. Knit all sts on needle 2. On needle 3, K1 K2tog knit to end (2 sts decreased).

Rnd 2: Knit.

Repeat rows 1 and 2 until 35 sts remain.

Rearrange the stitches onto the needles so that 10 sts are on needle 1, 10 sts are on needle 2, and 10 sts are on needle 3. Continue working in St st until piece measures 8", or approximately 2" shy of the total length of the foot.

Decrease for toe

The fabric created for the length of the foot must be decreased to fit snugly over the toe. Similar to the way that you decreased for the foot, you work a series of decreases for the toe.

Arrange the stitches on the three needles so that 9 sts are on needle 1, 17 sts are on needle 2, and 9 sts are on needle 3.

Rnd 1: Beg at marker, work to 3 sts before the end of needle 1: K2tog K1. At beg of needle 2: K1 SSK knit to 3 before end of the needle, K2tog K1. At beg of needle 3, K1 SSK and knit to end (4 sts decreased).

Rnd 2: Knit.

Repeat rows 1 and 2, decreasing every other rnd, until 15 sts remain. Then repeat row 1 only until 3 sts remain. Cut the yarn, leaving an 8" tail, and thread onto a tapestry needle. Thread the remaining stitches onto the needle and pull yarn through tightly. Weave in the ends.

Make the second sock to match.

Sandal Socks

Socks worn with sandals—at first glance, it's not a good fashion statement. Then again, when you start knitting your own socks, you may come to change your mind. These Sandal Socks are knit up in Koigu's **KPPPM** (a lusciously soft merino dyed in tons of colors) and feature a cabled honeycomb and a unique cabled rib throughout. What better way to show off your amazing handiwork than with sandals?

> **Tip**
>
> Although many sock yarns are machine washable, hand-knit socks should be washed by hand and dried flat. This will help extend their life and prevent them from felting during the wash.

below Flaunt your knitting prowess with these cabled socks.

Finished measurements: Cuff to heel: 10"; heel to toe: 10"; cuff circumference: 8.5"

Yarn: Koigu KPPPM 50g (175 yd.); 100% merino wool; shade P334; 3 skeins **Needles:** Set of 5 US size-2 double-pointed needles

Notions: Tapestry needle; cable needle; stitch marker **Gauge:** 28 sts and 36 rows = 4" in St st; 28 sts and 36 rows = 4" in cabled honeycomb; 28 sts and 36 rows = 4" in cabled rib

To save time and sanity:
TAKE TIME TO CHECK THE GAUGE.

Leg

CO 66 sts. Divide sts evenly across 3 dpns and join for working in the rnd by knitting the first stitch to the last, being careful not to twist sts. PM.

Cuff: Set up for ribbing as foll: P1 *K2 P2 repeat from * to end.

Next rnd: P2 *K2 P2 to end. Continue as set until cuff measures 3.5" (or longer, if desired).

Leg: Set up to work cables as follows: With needle 1, K16 P2; with needle 2, *K6 P2 repeat from * 3 more times; with needle 3, K16.

Next rnd: Beg with row 2 of cabled honeycomb chart, work chart twice over next 16 sts; P2; beg with row 2 of cabled rib chart, work chart four times over next 32 sts; beg with row 2 of cabled honeycomb chart, work chart twice over next 16 sts. Cont as charted in patt, rep rows 1–8 for each chart, three more times, ending on row 2 of charts. Piece should measure approximately 8.75" from beg.

Heel flap

Set up for working heel sts as foll: from marker, K16 P2. Turn. Sl 1 K1 purl 32 K2. Turn. Arrange rem sts among other two dpns and hold for instep. Working these 36 sts back and forth on one needle—slipping the first st of every row pwise—and beg with Row 4 of cabled honeycomb chart (working this chart only), cont in patt for 30 rows ending on a WS row.

Turn heel

Row 1: Knit to marker. K2 K2tog K1. Turn.

Row 2: P6 P2tog P1. Turn.

Row 3: Knit to 1 st before "gap," K2tog (one st from either side of gap) K1. Turn.

Row 4: Purl to 1 st before "gap," P2tog (one st from either side of gap) P1. Turn. Repeat rows 3 and 4 until all sts have been worked, ending on a WS row (20 sts). Note: the last two rows of the heel turn will end K2tog/P2tog—there will be no K1/P1 at the end of the row.

Gusset

With needle 1, knit across rem heel flap sts and continue up left-hand side of heel flap, picking up and knitting 15 selvedge sts. With needle 2, beg with row 3 of cabled rib chart, work across 32 sts held for instep. With needle 3, pick up and knit 15 selvedge sts down right-hand side of heel flap and, with same needle, knit to marker (80 sts). Sts should be arranged as foll: ½ of turned heel sts plus sts picked up from left side of heel flap on needle 1. Sts held from instep on needle 2. Sts picked up from right side of heel flap plus other ½ of turned heel sts on needle 3.

Decrease for foot

Rnd 1: Knit to 3 sts before end of needle 1, SSK, K1. Work in cabled rib patt across needle 2. At beg of needle 3, K1 K2tog, Knit to end (2 sts decreased).

Rnd 2: Knit to end of needle 1. Work in cabled rib patt across needle 2. Knit to end of needle 3. Rep rnds 1 and 2, decreasing 2 sts every other row, until 62 sts remain. Cont as set until sock measures 8" from base of heel (2" less than total length of foot).

Cabled honeycomb

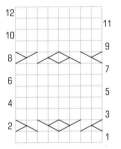

Cabled rib

Toe

Adjust sts for toe as foll: On needle 1, knit 15. On needle 2, knit 32. On needle 3, knit 15. Work toe decreases as foll (no longer working in patt st):

Rnd 1: Knit to 2 sts before end of needle 1, slip 2 sts tog knitwise; K1 st from needle 2 and pass the two slipped sts together over the knit st. Knit to 2 sts before end of needle 2. Repeat the process above, slipping two sts together from end of needle 2, knitting 1 st from needle 3, and passing the two slipped sts over the knit stitch. Knit to end (4 sts decreased).

Rnd 2: Knit.

Repeat rows 1 and 2 until 30 sts remain. Then repeat row 1 every row until 6 sts remain. Cut yarn and thread through to gather. Weave in the ends.

Make second sock to match.

	knit on a RS row, purl on a WS row
	purl on a RS row, knit on a WS row
	slip 4 sts to a cable needle and hold at front, K4, K4 from cable needle
	slip 3 sts to a cable needle and hold at front, K3, K3 from cable needle

Note: Charts are worked from right to left.

Medallion Mitts

Playing ball outside, eating on the go, driving: these can be clumsy experiences in the dead of winter without the use of all five digits. Better than gloves, these stylish, sturdy mitts offer your fingers full freedom, while keeping your hands warm. Worked up quickly in a unique hand-painted yarn, this pattern makes a great introduction to cables and offers an opportunity to practice picking up stitches, a skill often used in socks and sweaters.

Stitch Guide

Twisted rib (in the rnd)

(Multiples of 2)

Rnd 1: *K1tbl P1* to end.

Repeat row 1 for patt

below Fingerless mitts give your hands freedom to move.

Finished measurements: To fit an average man's hands: 6.5" long x 3" wide; thumb: 1" long x 1.5" wide **Yarn:** Artyarns Supermerino (104 yd.); 100% merino; shade: 106; 2 skeins **Needles:** Set of 4 US size-5 double-pointed needles **Notions:** Stitch marker; tapestry needle; cable needle; a small amount of light-colored worsted-weight scrap yarn **Gauge:** 20 sts and 30 rows = 4" in St st; medallion cable = 2.5"

To save time and sanity:

TAKE TIME TO CHECK THE GAUGE.

Left-hand mitt

CO 40 sts. Divide sts evenly onto three double-pointed needles as foll: 10 sts on needle 1, 20 sts on needle 2, and 10 sts on needle 3. Join, being careful not to twist sts and place marker (PM). Beg row 1 of twisted rib and repeat for 1.5".

Next row: Knit 11 sts, work first row of medallion cable chart, and knit 10 sts. Cont as charted, knitting the first 11 and last 10 sts of each rnd, until piece measures 4.5" from start.

Mark thumb placement

K1. Using scrap yarn, K 7 sts. Then slip these 7 sts back to the left-hand needle and reknit them using the Supermerino. Cont to work rnds as before, still working the medallion cable pattern, until piece measures 6.5" from start. Cast off loosely.

Thumb

Remove scrap yarn. Slip live sts onto two double-pointed needles. Join yarn and K7 sts. Pick up and knit 2 sts from the left side of the thumb opening. With this same needle, K5 sts on the next needle. With your empty needle, knit across the remaining 2 sts on this needle, and pick up and knit 2 sts from the right-hand side of the thumb opening (18 sts). K1 PM K6 K2tog K7 K2tog (16 sts). Work thumb in St st for 1" and cast off loosely. Sew in the ends.

Right-hand mitt

Work as for first mitt until thumb placement.

Next row: K32 sts in pattern. Using scrap yarn, K7 sts and then slip these sts back to the left-hand needle and reknit them using the Supermerino. Continue working mitt until piece measures 6.5" in length. Cast off loosely. Work thumb as above.

Medallion cable

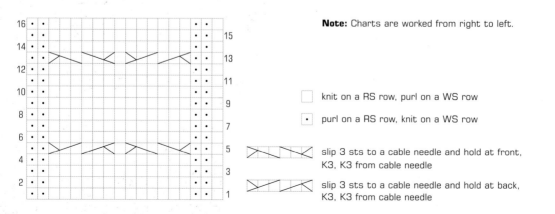

Note: Charts are worked from right to left.

☐ knit on a RS row, purl on a WS row

· purl on a RS row, knit on a WS row

⬚ slip 3 sts to a cable needle and hold at front, K3, K3 from cable needle

⬚ slip 3 sts to a cable needle and hold at back, K3, K3 from cable needle

Sweaters & Jackets

Casual Fridays Vest

History tells us that by the early Victorian era, long dress coats gave way to waistcoats as Western society became less formal and more forward-thinking. More recently, the corporate world's "Casual Fridays" took shape as a way to reward professionals at the end of a long week with a more comfortable dress code. The Casual Fridays Vest, worked up in the very popular Rowan Calmer, features shaping at the front cuffs and a clever combination of twisted knit stitches and purls.

Tip

Thrift and antique stores are a great source of unusual and unique buttons. Don't be afraid to rummage through old clothes and buy a garment simply to rip off the buttons.

below A classic vest signals the end of the working week.

Finished measurements: 40" (45½", 48", 53½", 61½") **Yarn:** Rowan Calmer 50 g (175 yd.); 75% cotton, 25% acrylic microfiber; shade: 480 Peacock; 7 (9, 9, 11, 14) balls **Needles:** 24", US size-7 circular needle **Notions:** Tapestry needle; stitch markers; six 1" metal buttons **Gauge:** 21 sts and 32 rows = 4" in St st; 24 sts and 34 rows = 4" in Swedish check pattern

To save time and sanity:
TAKE TIME TO CHECK THE GAUGE.

Back

CO 120 (136, 144, 160, 184) sts.

Work in Swedish check patt (see page 82) until piece measures 14" (14½", 15", 16", 17") from CO, ending with a WS row.

Shape armholes: BO 6 (7, 9, 9, 12) sts at beg of next 2 rows, then BO 3 (3, 4, 4, 8) sts at beg of foll 2 rows. (102 [116, 118, 134, 144] sts rem.) Dec 1 st each end of needle every RS row 5 (5, 5, 9, 9) times. (92 [106, 108, 116, 126] sts rem.) Work even until armholes measure 9½" (11", 11½", 13", 15"), ending with a WS row.

Shape shoulders: BO 8 (8, 8, 9, 9) sts at beg of next 4 rows, then BO 7 (8, 8, 8, 9) sts at beg of foll 2 rows. (46 [58, 60, 64, 72] sts rem.) BO rem sts.

Right front

CO 11 (11, 15, 15, 19) sts. K11 (11, 15, 15. 19) tbl.

Shape lower edge as foll:

Row 1: (WS) Sl 1 P1 M1, purl to end.

Row 2: Sl 1 K2 tbl *P2 K2 tbl, rep from * to last st, M1 K1.

Row 3: Sl 1 P1 M1 P2 *K2 P2, rep from * to last st, P1.

Row 4: Sl 1, knit tbl to last 2 sts, M1 K1 M1 K1.

Row 5: Sl 1 P1 M1, purl to end.

Row 6: Sl 1 P2 *K2 tbl P2, rep from * to last 2 sts, K1 tbl M1 K1.

Row 7: Sl 1 M1 *P2 K2, rep from * to last st, P1.

Row 8: Sl 1, knit tbl to last 2 sts, M1 K1 M1 K1.

Cont in patt as set, inc 1 st at end of each RS row, at beg of each WS row, and an additional st on the 4th and 8th row of each patt rep, working new sts into patt, until there are 60 (68, 72, 80, 92) sts on the needle (Note: for size 40", there will only be 1 inc on last row of last rep.) Work even in Swedish check patt, beg with row 2 (8, 8, 6, 5), until piece measures 14" (14½", 15", 16", 17") from end of lower edge shaping, ending with a RS row.

Shape armhole: BO 6 (7, 9, 9, 12) sts at beg of next row, then BO 3 (3, 4, 4, 8) sts at beg of next WS row. (51 [58, 59, 67, 72] sts rem.) Dec 1 st at armhole edge (end of RS rows) every other row 5 (5, 5, 9, 9) times. (46 [53, 54, 58, 63] sts rem.) Work even until armhole measures 2" (2¼", 2½", 3¾", 5)", ending with a WS row.

Shape neck: Dec 1 st at neck edge every other row 18 (23, 24, 26, 29) times. (28 [30, 30, 32, 34] sts rem.) Work even until armhole measures 9½" (11", 11½", 13", 15")", ending with a RS row.

Shape shoulder: At beg of WS rows, BO 8 (8, 8, 9, 9) sts 2 times, then BO 7 (8, 8, 8, 9) sts once. (5 [6, 6, 6, 7] sts rem.) BO rem sts.

Left front

CO 11 (11, 15, 15, 19) sts. K11 (11, 15, 15, 19) tbl.

Shape lower edge as foll:

Row 1: (WS) Sl 1, purl to last st, M1 P1.

Row 2: Sl 1 M1 K2 tb1 *P2 K2 tbl, rep from * to last st, K1.

Row 3: Sl 1 P2 *K2 P2, rep from * to last 2 sts, K1 M1 K1.

Row 4: Sl 1 M1 K1 M1, knit tbl to end.

Row 5: Sl 1, purl to last st, M1 P1.

Row 6: Sl 1 M1 P3 *K2 tbl P2, rep from * to last st, K1.

Row 7: Sl 1 K2 *P2 K2, rep from * to last 3 sts, P2 M1 K1.

Row 8: Sl 1 M1 K1 M1, knit tbl to end.

Cont in patt as set, inc 1 st at beg of each RS row, at end of each WS row, and an additional st on the 4th and 8th row of each patt rep, working new sts into patt, until there are 60 (68, 72, 80, 92) sts on the needle. (Note: for size 40", there will only be 1 inc on last row of last rep.) Work even in Swedish check patt, beg with row 2 (8, 8, 6, 5), until piece measures 14" (14½", 15", 16", 17") from end of lower edge shaping, ending with a WS row.

Shape armhole: BO 6 (7, 9, 9, 12) sts at beg of next row, then BO 3 (3, 4, 4, 8) sts at beg of next RS row. (51 [58, 59, 67, 72] sts rem.) Dec 1 st at armhole edge (beg of RS rows) every other row 5 (5, 5, 9, 9) times. (46 [53, 54, 58, 63] sts rem.) Work even until armhole measures 2" (2 ¼", 2 ½", 3 ¾", 5"), ending with a WS row.

Shape neck: Dec 1 st at neck edge every other row 18 (23, 24, 26, 29) times. (28 [30, 30, 32, 34] sts rem.) Work even until armhole measures 9½" (11", 11½", 13", 15"), ending with a WS row.

Shape shoulder: At beg of RS rows, BO 8 (8, 8, 9, 9) sts 2 times, then BO 7 (8, 8, 8, 9) sts once. (5 [6, 6, 6, 7] sts rem.) BO rem sts.

Finishing

With yarn and a tapestry needle, sew the shoulder and side seams. Weave in the ends.

Lower border and button band

Beg at left front lower edge, with RS facing, pick up and knit 35 (40, 42, 46, 54) sts across left front lower edge, 90 (102, 108, 120, 138) sts across back, and 35 (40, 42, 46, 54) sts across right front lower edge (160 [182, 192, 212, 246] sts). Work in garter st for 1". BO.

Beg at right front lower edge, with RS facing, pick up and knit 6 sts in garter ridges of lower border, 160 (172, 178, 194, 216) sts up right front to shoulder, 28 (36, 38, 40, 45) sts across back neck, PM, 160 (172, 178, 194, 216) sts down left front to lower border, 6 sts in garter ridges of lower border (360 [392, 406, 440, 489] sts). Work 5 rows in garter st, ending with a WS row.

Next row (buttonhole row): Knit to marker, *K2tog, yo (twice), K19 (21, 22, 24, 27); rep from * 5 more times, knit to end of row.

Next row: drop second yo from needle. (Do not work into second yo.) Work even in garter st until band measures 1". BO all sts loosely. Weave in the ends. Sew buttons onto right front band opposite buttonhole.

Garment measurements

The schematic below acts as an illustration of all of the key measurements for the Casual Fridays Vest. Refer to it to gain an idea of the shape and layout of the finished garment.

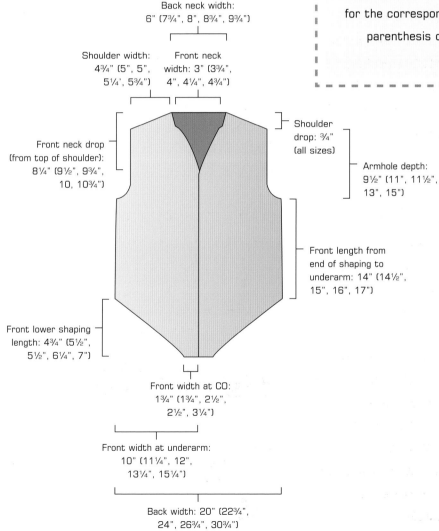

Back neck width:
6" (7¾", 8", 8¾", 9¾")

Shoulder width:
4¾" (5", 5",
5¼', 5¾")

Front neck
width: 3" (3¾",
4", 4¼", 4¾")

Shoulder
drop: ¾"
(all sizes)

Front neck drop
(from top of shoulder):
8¼" (9½", 9¾",
10, 10¾")

Armhole depth:
9½" (11", 11½",
13", 15")

Front length from
end of shaping to
underarm: 14" (14½",
15", 16", 17")

Front lower shaping
length: 4¾" (5½",
5½", 6¼", 7")

Front width at CO:
1¾" (1¾", 2½",
2½", 3¼")

Front width at underarm:
10" (11¼", 12",
13¼", 15¼")

Back width: 20" (22¾",
24", 26¾", 30¾")

Bootcut Sweater

Bootcut jeans made their comeback in the late 1990s. The slits in the cuff were all about allowing your jeans to fit easily over your boots without making anything look too tight or uncomfortable. The Bootcut Sweater offers the same benefits of the pant—offering deep slits in the waist cuff, sleeves, and collar. Based on Elizabeth Zimmermann's Percentage System, the sweater fits snugly over your torso and arms, and leaves a bit of extra fabric at all the right junctures to ensure a great fit.

below The bootcut sweater offers both comfort and style.

Finished measurements: 42" (44", 48", 52", 60") **Yarn:** Mountain Colors Weavers Wool Quarters 4 oz (350 yd.); 100% wool; shade: Pheasant; 4 (5, 5, 6, 7) skeins **Needles:** 16" and 32", US size-7 circular needles **Notions:** Tapestry needle; stitch markers; large stitch holder **Gauge:** 20 sts and 28 rows = 4" in St st

To save time and sanity:
TAKE TIME TO CHECK THE GAUGE.

Body cuff

(lower edge of body)

With 16" needle, CO 100 (105, 115, 125, 145) sts. Work in garter st for 8 rows, ending with a WS row. Change to St st, maintaining a 3-st garter st border at beg and end of row, and work even until piece measures 2½" from CO, ending with a WS row. Break yarn and set aside. With 32" needle, make second cuff to match, but do not break yarn.

Body

Join the cuffs and work in the rnd.

With 32" needle, knit 1 RS row of second cuff, leaving last st unworked. Then, with RS facing, using last st from this needle and first st from 16" needle, K2tog. Knit sts from the 16" needle to the 32" needle, leaving last st unworked. Sl last st kwise, knit first st of row to join for working in the rnd, and pass the slipped st over the knit st (198 [208, 228, 248, 288] sts). PM for beg of rnd.

Next rnd: Work in St st, inc 12 sts evenly spaced (210 [220, 240, 260, 300] sts).

Next rnd: K105 (110, 120, 130, 150), PM for right underarm, knit to end of rnd. Work even in St st until piece measures 15½" (16, 16½", 17, 17½"), ending 5 (5, 6, 7, 8) sts before end of last rnd.

Divide for front and back: BO 10 (10, 12, 14, 16) sts, removing marker, work in St st to 5 (5, 6, 7, 8) sts before second marker, BO 10 (10, 12, 14, 16) sts, removing marker, work in St st to end of rnd. (190 [200, 216, 232, 268] sts rem.) Set aside while working sleeves.

Sleeves

With 16" needle, CO 45 (45, 49, 53, 55) sts. Working back and forth, work in garter st for 8 rows, ending with a WS row. Change to St st, maintaining a 3-st garter st border at beg and end of row, and work even until piece measures 2½" from CO, ending with a WS row. Knit to last st and then, using first and last sts of row, K2tog to join for working in the rnd. PM for beg of rnd (44 [44, 48, 52, 54] sts). Discontinue garter st borders; work all sts in St st.

Next rnd: Inc 6 sts evenly spaced (50 [50, 54, 58, 60] sts).

Work even in St st for 3 rnds.

Next rnd: K1 M1 knit to last st M1 K1 (52 [52, 56, 60, 62] sts).

Work 6 (6, 6, 5, 5) rnds even. Rep the last 7 (7, 7, 6, 6) rnds 12 (13, 14, 15, 16) more times (76 [78, 84, 90, 94] sts).

Work even in St st until piece measures 17½" (18", 19", 19½", 20") from CO, ending 5 (5, 6, 7, 8) sts before marker on last rnd. BO 10 (10, 12, 14, 16) sts; place rem sts on holder. (66 [68, 72, 76, 78] sts rem.) Break yarn. Make a second sleeve to match, but do not place sts onto a holder and do not break yarn.

Yoke

With 32" needle, K66 (68, 72, 76, 78) sleeve sts, K48 (50, 54, 58, 67) front sts, PM for center front, knit rem 47 (50, 54, 58, 67) front sts, K66 (68, 72, 76, 78) held sleeve sts, PM, K95 (100, 108, 116, 134) back sts, PM for beg of rnd (322 [336, 360, 384, 424] sts). Working in the rnd, dec 2 (1, 0, 4, 9) st(s) evenly spaced on next rnd. (320 [335, 360, 380, 415] sts rem.) Work even in St st until yoke measures 3" (3", 3", 3½", 4") from join.

Dec rnd 1: *K3 K2tog, rep from * to end of rnd. (256 [268, 288, 304, 332] sts rem.)

Divide for placket: Knit to 4 sts before center front marker. BO 8 sts, removing marker, then knit arnd to center front. CO 4 sts. (252 [264, 284, 300, 328] sts rem.) Beg working back and forth in rows.

Next row: (WS) K4, purl to end, CO 4 sts (256 [268, 288, 304, 332] sts).

Next row: Knit.

Next row: K4, purl to last 4 sts, K4. Cont as set, maintaining a 4-st garter st border on each side of center front, until yoke measures 5½" (5½", 5½", 6", 6½"), ending with a WS row.

Dec row 2: K4 *K2 K2tog, rep from * to last 4 sts, K4. (194 [203, 218, 230, 251] sts rem.) Work even until yoke measures 7½" (7½", 8", 8½", 9¼"), ending with a WS row.

Dec row 3: K4 *K1 K2tog, rep from * to last 4 sts, K4. (132 [138, 148, 156, 170] sts rem.) Work even until yoke measures 10" (10", 10½", 11", 11¾"), ending with a WS row.

Raise back neck: Knit to 1 st before second marker (back of left sleeve). Sl next st pwise, bring yarn to front of work, return slipped st to left-hand needle and bring yarn to back of work (1 st wrapped RS). Turn work.

Purl to 1 st before next marker (back of right sleeve). Bring yarn to back of work, sl next st pwise, bring yarn to front of work and return slipped st to left-hand needle (1 st wrapped WS). Turn work.

Knit to 5 sts before marker, work 1 st wrapped RS as described above. Turn work. Knit to 5 sts before marker, work 1 st wrapped WS as described above. Turn work.

*Knit to first wrapped st and knit wrap tog with wrapped st as foll: sl wrapped st to right-hand needle, lift wrap onto left-hand needle, return wrapped st to left-hand needle and K2tog. Rep from * for second wrapped st on this row; knit to end.

Next row: (WS) K4, *purl to first wrapped st and purl wrap tog with wrapped st as foll: reach right needle to RS, then up into wrap from below, place wrap onto left-hand needle and P2tog. Rep from * for second wrapped st; purl to last 4 sts, K4.

Dec row 4: K4 (4, 5, 4, 4), *K1 K2tog; rep from * to last 5 (5, 5, 5, 4) sts, K5 (5, 5, 5, 4). (91 [95, 102, 107, 116] sts rem.) BO all sts.

Neckband

With RS facing, pick up and knit 68 (71, 76, 80, 86) sts around neck, beg and ending at front slit. Work in garter st for 6 rows. BO all sts.

Finishing

Weave in all the ends. With a tapestry needle and yarn, loosely whipstitch underarm seam. Sew CO sts to BO sts at lower edge of each front placket.

Garment measurements

At first glance, a sweater schematic gives more information than you'd ever want to know. However, keep in mind that it exists as an extra tool to help you ensure good fit—and that most sweaters can be made by just working with the measurements included in the pattern text.

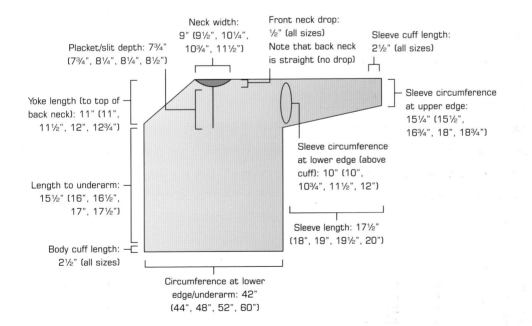

Neck width:
9" (9½", 10¼", 10¾", 11½")

Front neck drop:
½" (all sizes)
Note that back neck is straight (no drop)

Placket/slit depth: 7¾"
(7¾", 8¼", 8¼", 8½")

Sleeve cuff length:
2½" (all sizes)

Yoke length (to top of back neck): 11" (11", 11½", 12", 12¾")

Sleeve circumference at upper edge:
15¼" (15½", 16¾", 18", 18¾")

Sleeve circumference at lower edge (above cuff): 10" (10", 10¾", 11½", 12")

Length to underarm: 15½" (16", 16½", 17", 17½")

Sleeve length: 17½" (18", 19", 19½", 20")

Body cuff length: 2½" (all sizes)

Circumference at lower edge/underarm: 42" (44", 48", 52", 60")

Hooded Alpaca Parka

Picture it: an October morning, you're up early and ready to go for a run—or maybe just walk the dog. It's too chilly outside for a sweatshirt and too warm for a coat. What do you wear? Made from 100% alpaca, a fiber warmer than wool and at least as waterproof, the Hooded Alpaca Parka is exactly what you need. With sleeve cuffs that fold over to make fingerless mitts, a dual-direction zipper, and optional sew-on fluorescent fabric, this garment's got it all. Take that, Mother Nature!

below The perfect hooded parka for a cool fall day.

Finished measurements: 40½" (44¼", 48", 51¾", 60½") **Yarn:** Blue Sky Alpacas Sportweight 50 g (110 yd.); 100% alpaca; shade: 73 Tarnished Gold; 14 (17, 19, 21, 26) hanks **Needles:** 16" and 32", US size-5 circular needles; set of 4 US size-5 double-pointed needles **Notions:** Tapestry needle; stitch markers; 1 stitch holder; 22" (24", 26", 26", 28") dual-direction zipper; sewing thread to match yarn; sewing needle; 12" of 30"-wide lemon-yellow reflective fabric (optional)
Gauge: 22 sts and 30 rows = 4" in St st; 22.5 sts and 36 rows = 4" in 5 x 2 broken rib pattern

To save time and sanity:
TAKE TIME TO CHECK THE GAUGE.

Body

With 32" circular needle, CO 52 (57, 60, 66, 76) sts, PM, CO 12 (12, 16, 16, 20) sts, PM, CO 100 (111, 118, 127, 148) sts, PM, CO 12 (12, 16, 16, 20) sts, PM, CO 52 (57, 60, 66, 76) sts. (228 [249, 270, 291, 340] sts total.)

Beg 5 x 2 broken rib pattern as foll:

Row 1: (RS) Sl 1 pwise P2 *K5 P2, rep from * to last st, K1.

Row 2: Sl 1 pwise, purl to end of row.

Rep rows 1 and 2 until piece measures 14½" (16", 16½", 17", 18") from CO, ending with a RS row.

Next row: (WS) Sl 1 pwise, purl to marker, BO 12 (12, 16, 16, 20) sts pwise, removing markers, purl to marker, BO 12 (12, 16, 16, 20) sts pwise, removing markers, purl to end of row. (204 [225, 238, 259, 300] sts rem.) Leave piece on needle and set aside.

Sleeves

With double-pointed needles, CO 56 (56, 63, 63, 70) sts. PM and join for working in the rnd, being careful not to twist.

Rnd 1: Knit.

Rnd 2: M1 for "seam" st, PM, *K5 P2, rep from * around (57 [57, 64, 64, 71] sts).

Rnd 3: Knit.

Rnd 4: K1 *K5 P2, rep from * around.

Rep rnds 3 and 4 until piece measures 2" from CO, ending with rnd 3.

Inc rnd: K1, sl m, M1, work in patt to marker, M1, sl m.

Work even for 7 (6, 7, 5, 5) rnds. Rep the last 8 (7, 8, 6, 6) rnds 13 (17, 16, 20, 24) more times, working new sts into patt, and changing to circular needle when convenient (85 [93, 98, 106, 121] sts).

Work even until piece measures 17¾" (19", 20¼", 20½", 21") from CO, ending with an even-numbered (K5, P2) rnd, and ending last rnd 6 (6, 8, 8, 10) sts before end of rnd. BO 13 (13, 17, 17, 21) sts, removing markers, and work to end. (72 [80, 81, 89, 100] sts rem.)

Place sts on holder, break yarn, and work a second sleeve to match. When the second sleeve is complete, break the yarn, but do not remove the sleeve from the needle.

Join sleeves to body: With RS facing and cont in patt as established, work 52 (57, 60, 66, 76) sts of right front, PM, work 72 (80, 81, 89, 100) held sleeve sts, PM, work 100 (111, 118, 127, 148) sts of back, PM, work 72 (80, 81, 89, 100) held sleeve sts, PM, work 52 (57, 60, 66, 76) sts of left front. (348 [385, 400, 437, 500] sts total.)

Slip the first stitch pwise; purl 1 (WS) row.

Work raglan decreases: Dec row: (RS) *Work in patt to 2 sts before marker, SSK, sl m, K2tog, rep from * for each marker, work in patt to end of row. Work 3 rows even. Rep the last 4 rows 1 (3, 5, 3, 2) more time(s). (332 [353, 352, 405, 476] sts rem.) Rep dec row every other row 32 (34, 32, 38, 45) times. (76 [81, 96, 101, 116] sts rem.) BO all sts.

Hood

With 32" circular needle and RS facing, beg at right front upper edge, pick up and knit 40 (42, 50, 53, 61) sts to center back, PM, pick up and knit 40 (42, 50, 53, 61) sts to left front edge. (80 [84, 100, 106, 122] sts total.)

Next row: Increase 10 sts evenly across rnd.

Next row: (WS) Purl.

Rep last two rows 2 (2, 2, 1, 0) more times. 110 (114, 120, 126, 132) sts total. Work even in St st until piece measures 12" (14", 14½", 15", 16½") from pick-up row, ending with a WS row.

Next row: Dec 10 sts evenly across rnd.

Next row: Purl.

Rep last two rows 2 (2, 2, 1, 0) times more. 80 (84, 100, 106, 122) sts total.

Dec row: (RS) Knit to 3 sts before marker, ssk, K1, sl m, K1 K2tog, knit to end of row. Rep dec row every other row 5 more times. (68 [72, 88, 94, 110] sts rem.) Sl 34 (36, 44, 47, 55) sts to 16" circular needle. With RS tog, BO using the three-needle BO.

Cuff

With double-pointed needles and RS facing, beg at "seam" st, pick up and knit 50 (50, 56, 56, 62) sts around edge of sleeve. PM and join for working in the rnd. Work in St st for 1½", ending last rnd 2 sts before marker. BO 4 sts, knit to end of rnd. (46 [46, 52, 52, 58] sts rem.) Working back and forth, cont in St st until cuff measures 2½" from pick-up rnd, ending with a RS row. CO 4 sts using the knit-on method, PM and join for working in the rnd (50 [50, 56, 56, 62] sts). Work in St st until cuff measures 3½" from pick-up rnd. BO all sts loosely.

Finishing

Weave in all the ends. With a tapestry needle and yarn, loosely whipstitch the underarm seam. Sew the zipper to the opening at front of sweater (see the tutorial on the facing page).

To attach the reflective fabric for cyclists and runners, cut the fabric into three 6"-wide strips: one strip as wide as your sweater back 1" below sleeve join, and two strips as wide as the distance from the front opening to the underarm. Hand sew the fabric to the knitting using sewing thread.

Garment measurements

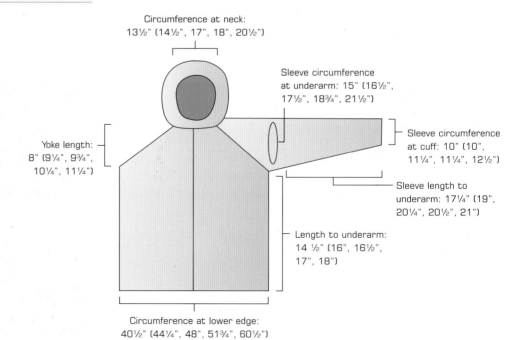

Circumference at neck:
13½" (14½", 17", 18", 20½")

Sleeve circumference at underarm: 15" (16½", 17½", 18¾", 21½")

Sleeve circumference at cuff: 10" (10", 11¼", 11¼", 12½")

Yoke length:
8" (9¼", 9¾", 10¼", 11¼")

Sleeve length to underarm: 17¼" (19", 20¼", 20½", 21")

Length to underarm:
14 ½" (16", 16½", 17", 18")

Circumference at lower edge:
40½" (44¼", 48", 51¾", 60½")

Attaching a zipper to knitted fabric

Known for providing easy access and sporty style, the zipper is one of the most guy-friendly closures out there. While installing a zipper can be a challenge at times, many find it easier to sew it in place by hand than by machine.

1. With the RS of the garment facing and the zipper closed (in one piece), attach the zipper to the sweater—lining up the bottom and top of the zipper with the bottom cuff and collar top of the parka closure using safety pins. The zipper should rest underneath the selvedge stitches (see page 120) at the edge of the opening.

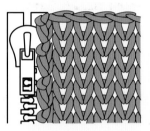

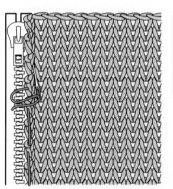

2. Using a contrasting color of sewing thread, baste the zipper onto the garment, sewing through the zipper and the selvedge stitches, pulling the needle and thread through to the WS, and reinserting it to the front of the work and pulling through using a series of long, loose stitches. Sew both sides of the zipper to the garment in this fashion.

3. Turn the garment inside out, so that the WS of the sweater is facing. Using a thread that complements the color of the yarn for your garment, sew the zipper in place, using a series of short stitches up and down both sides of the zipper. Note: if you're working on an item with no WS (for instance, the closure for a bag), it's okay to open the zipper up slightly at the top to sew and catch the needle and thread.

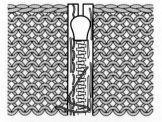

4. Once the zipper has been sewn in place on both sides, remove the long stitches used to baste the zipper to the garment.

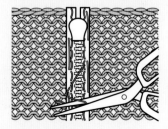

Argyle Pullover Vest

Argyle, inspired by **Scotsmen's** plaid kilts cut on the bias, didn't actually make its way into popular culture until the **1940s**. Since then, argyle has been in and out of style—much like the sweater vest itself. Now it's trendier than ever before. Worked up in intarsia, the Argyle Pullover Vest is knitted with Malabrigo Merino, a super-soft hand-dyed merino from South America, which gives a modern feel to a classic design.

> **Tip**
>
> Don't worry about the orange outlined diamond pattern in the argyle—duplicate stitch is a perfect way to add small amounts of color (or even to fix a mistake in the pattern) after a project is complete.

below Multicolored yarns give argyle a new look.

Finished measurements: 38" (42", 45½", 49", 52½", 59½") **Yarn:** Malabrigo Kettle Dyed Pure Merino Wool 100 g (216 yd.); shade: Stonechat (Color 173), MC: 3 (4, 4, 5, 5, 6) skeins CC1: 1 skein CC2: 1 skein; shade: Olive (Color 56) 1 skein (CC1); shade: Sunset (Color 96),1 skein (CC2) **Needles:** 24", US size-9 circular needle **Notions:** Tapestry needle; stitch marker; removable markers; large stitch holder **Gauge:** 18 sts and 27 rows = 4" in St st.

To save time and sanity:
TAKE TIME TO CHECK THE GAUGE.

Note: Slip first st of every row pwise.

Back

With MC, CO 86 (94, 102, 110, 118, 134) sts. Sl 1, work in K2 P2 rib to last st, K1. Work even for 2½", ending with a WS row. Change to St st and work even until piece measures 14" (14", 14½", 15", 15½", 16½") from CO, ending with a WS row.

Shape armholes: BO 4 (4, 4, 6, 7, 9) sts at beg of next 2 rows, then BO 3 (3, 3, 4, 4, 6) sts at beg of foll 2 rows. (72 [80, 88, 90, 96, 104] sts rem.)

Dec row: (RS) K1, ssk, knit to last 3 sts, K2tog, K1. Rep dec row every other row 4 (4, 4, 4, 6, 6) more times. (62 [70, 78, 80, 82, 90] sts rem.) Work even until armholes measure 9½" (9¾", 11", 12", 12½", 14½"), ending with a WS row.

Shape shoulders: BO 6 (7, 8, 8, 8, 8) sts at beg of next 2 rows, then BO 5 (7, 7, 7, 7, 8) sts at beg of foll 2 rows, then BO 5 (6, 7, 7, 7, 8) sts at beg of foll 2 rows. (30 [30, 34, 36, 38, 42] sts rem.) BO rem sts.

Front

With MC, CO 86 (94, 102, 110, 118, 134) sts. Sl 1, work in K2 P2 rib to last st, K1. Work even for 2½", ending with a WS row. Change to St st. K43 (47, 51, 55, 59, 67), M1, knit to end of row (87 [95, 103, 111, 119, 135] sts). Work even in St st until piece measures 9" (9", 11", 11¾", 12½", 14½") from CO, ending with a WS row. Beg chart: K18 (22, 26, 30, 34, 42), PM, work row 1 of Argyle chart, working only the MC and CC1 sts, PM, knit to end of row. Cont as established through chart row 26. On chart row 27, K43 (47, 51, 55, 59, 67), place removable marker in next st to mark center of diamond, knit to end of row. Work even until piece measures 14" (14", 14½", 15", 15½", 16½") from CO, ending with a WS row.

Shape armholes: Cont with chart patt on center sts, BO 4 (4, 4, 6, 7, 9) sts at beg of next 2 rows, then BO 3 (3, 3, 4, 4, 6) sts at beg of foll 2 rows. (73 [81, 89, 91, 97, 105] sts rem.) Dec 1 st at each end of needle every RS row (as for back) 5 (5, 5, 5, 7, 7) times. (63 [71, 79, 81, 83, 91] sts rem.) Work even to end of chart, then work even in MC until armholes measure 3" (3", 4½", 4¾", 5", 6"), ending with a WS row.

Divide for front neck: K31 (35, 39, 40, 41, 45). Place rem 32 (36, 40, 41, 42, 46) sts on holder. Turn and work 1 (WS) row. Dec 1 st at neck edge every RS row 12 (11, 16, 16, 17, 17) times. (19 [24, 23, 24, 24, 28] sts rem.) Work 3 rows even. Dec 1 st at neck edge on next row. Rep

the llast 4 rows 2 (3, 0, 1, 1, 3) more times. (16 [20, 22, 22, 22, 24] sts rem.) Work even in St st until armholes measure 9½" (9¾", 11", 12", 12½", 14½"), ending with a WS row.
Shape shoulders: BO 6 (7, 8, 8, 8, 8) sts at beg of next row, then BO 5 (7, 7, 7, 7, 8) sts at beg of foll RS row, then BO 5 (6, 7, 7, 7, 8) sts at beg of foll RS row.

Leave first held st (center st) on holder. With RS facing, join MC to rem 31 (35, 39, 40, 41, 45) sts. Work 2 rows even. Dec 1 st at neck edge every RS row 12 (11, 16, 16, 17, 17) times. (19 [24, 23, 24, 24, 28] sts rem.) Work 3 rows even. Dec 1 st at neck edge on next row. Rep the last 4 rows 2 (3, 0, 1, 1, 3) more times. (16 [20, 22, 22, 22, 24] sts rem.) Work even in St st until armholes measure 9½" (9¾", 11", 12", 12½", 14½"), ending with a RS row. BO 6 (7, 8, 8, 8, 8) sts at beg of next row, then BO 5 (7, 7, 7, 7, 8) sts at beg of foll WS row, then BO 5 (6, 7, 7, 7, 8) sts at beg of foll WS row.

Finishing

With RS tog, sew the shoulder seams.
Sew the side seams.

Neckband

With RS facing and MC, beg at right shoulder seam, pick up and knit 30 (30, 34, 34, 38, 42) sts across back neck, pick up and knit 24 (24, 24, 28, 28, 32) sts down left front neck, knit single held center front st and mark this st with a removable marker, pick up and knit 24 (24, 24, 28, 28, 32) sts up right front neck (79 [79, 83, 91, 95, 107] sts). PM and join for working in the rnd. Work neckband as foll:
Set-up rnd: K2 *P2 K2, rep from * to marked st, knit marked st, **K2 P2, rep from ** to end of rnd.
Rnd 1: Work in rib to 1 st before marked st, sl 2 sts tog kwise, K1, P2sso, work in rib to end of rnd (2 sts decreased).
Rnd 2: Work in rib to marked st, knit marked st, work in rib to end of rnd. Rep rnds 1 and 2 until neckband measures 1", ending with rnd 1. BO all sts.

Armbands

With MC and RS facing, pick up and knit 56 (56, 64, 72, 72, 84) sts around armhole. PM and join for working in the rnd. Work even in K2 P2 rib for 1". BO all sts. Rep for other armhole.

Argyle pattern

With CC2 and beg at marker for center of diamond, duplicate st center st. Using this st as a guide and following chart, duplicate st in Argyle pattern as shown. Weave in all the ends.

Garment measurements

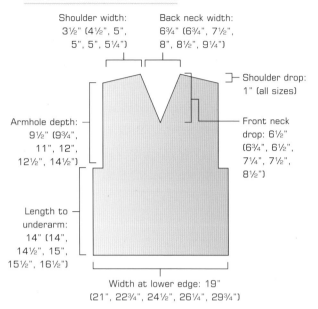

Shoulder width:
3½" (4½", 5", 5", 5", 5¼")

Back neck width:
6¾" (6¾", 7½", 8", 8½", 9¼")

Shoulder drop: 1" (all sizes)

Armhole depth:
9½" (9¾", 11", 12", 12½", 14½")

Front neck drop: 6½" (6¾", 6½", 7¼", 7½", 8½")

Length to underarm:
14" (14", 14½", 15", 15½", 16½")

Width at lower edge: 19" (21", 22¾", 24½", 26¼", 29¾")

Argyle chart

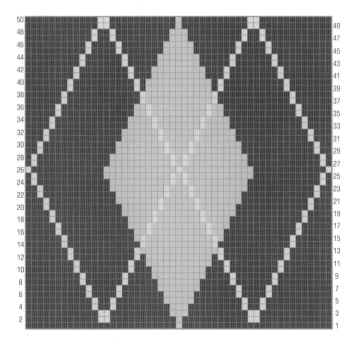

■ CC1

■ MC

▨ CC2 (work in duplicate stitch)

Note: RS rows are worked right to left, WS rows are worked left to right

Duplicate stitch

Duplicate stitch is a great trick—pulled from needlepoint—used to replace one stitch with another of a different color after the garment has been bound off. The technique is really useful for adding little bits of color, such as the orange diamonds on the Argyle Vest, and for correcting mistakes in color work.

To make a duplicate stitch, you will need a short length of yarn (the color you'd like to show in the final piece) and a tapestry needle. Thread the yarn on the needle and find the stitch (or stitches) to be duplicated on the work.

Tip

When duplicating more than one stitch in a garment, try to work all the stitches in the same row before moving onto other rows in the area of color.

1. Insert the tapestry needle through the center of the stitch below the one to be duplicated, from back to front.

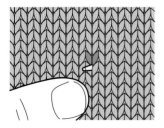

2. Next, working from right to left, insert the tapestry needle under both loops of the stitch above the one being duplicated. Pull the yarn through.

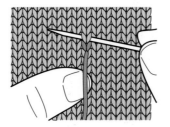

3. Then, working from front to back, insert the tapestry needle through the same hole that the needle came through initially. Give the yarn and needle a little tug to secure it in place, and begin working the next stitch to be duplicated.

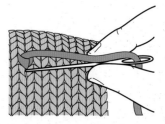

Tribal Sweater

Tattoos serve many purposes. As marks of status, sexual enticements, and rites of passage, tattoos hold deep and often personal symbolism for the owner. The Tribal Sweater, inspired by tattoos popular at present, contains two charts worked in intarsia featuring tribal motifs. To make the sweater, use the two charts below—or follow our tip to construct your own and make the sweater design unique.

> **Tip**
>
> To make your own charts, pick up some graph paper and a pencil with an eraser, and begin sketching motifs that you might like to use. Fill in the squares with color according to where the lines of your drawing fall.

below An intarsia design looks striking in white on black.

Finished measurements: 40½" (44", 48", 52", 60") **Yarn:** Cascade 220 100 g (220 yds.); 100% wool; shade: Black #8555, MC: 5 (6, 6, 7, 8) skeins CC: 1 skein; shade: Natural #8010, 1 skein (CC) **Needles:** 16" and 24", US size-8 circular needles **Notions:** Tapestry needle; stitch markers **Gauge:** 17 sts and 24 rows = 4" in St st.

To save time and sanity:

TAKE TIME TO CHECK THE GAUGE.

Note: For whole garment, slip first st of every row pwise to ease finishing.

Back

With MC, CO 86 (94, 102, 110, 128) sts. Work even in St st until piece measures 14½" (15", 15½", 16", 17") from CO, ending with a WS row.

Shape armholes: BO 4 (4, 5, 6, 8) sts at beg of next 2 rows, then BO 3 (3, 4, 5, 6) sts at beg of foll 2 rows. (72 [80, 84, 88, 100] sts rem.) Dec 1 st each end of needle every RS row 4 (5, 5, 4, 6) times. (64 [70, 74, 80, 88] sts rem.) Work even in St st until armholes measure 9½" (10", 10½", 11", 12"), ending with a WS row.

Shape shoulders: BO 9 (10, 10, 11, 12) sts at beg of next 2 rows, then BO 8 (10, 10, 11, 12) sts at beg of foll 2 rows. (30 [30, 34, 36, 40] sts rem.) BO rem sts.

Front

Work as for back until piece measures 11" (12", 13", 14", 16") from CO, ending with a WS row.

Beg chart: K12 (16, 20, 24, 33), PM, work row 1 of Chart A, PM, knit to end of row. Cont as established through end of chart. At the same time, when piece measures 14½" (15", 15½", 16", 17") from CO, ending with a WS row, shape armholes as for back. Work even until armholes measure 7½" (8", 8½", 9", 10"), ending with a WS row.

Shape neck: K24 (27, 27, 30, 34), join second ball of yarn and BO 16 (16, 20, 20, 20) sts, knit to end of row. (24 [27, 27, 30, 34] sts rem each side.) Working each side separately, purl 1 row. At each neck edge, BO 3 (3, 3, 4, 5) sts once, then BO 2 (2, 2, 2, 3) sts once, then dec 1 st every other row 2 times. (17 [20, 20, 22, 24] sts rem each side.) Work even until armholes measure 9½" (10", 10½", 11", 12"), ending with a WS row.

Shape shoulders: At each shoulder edge, BO 9 (10, 10, 11, 12) sts once, then BO 8 (10, 10, 11, 12) sts once.

Sleeves

With MC, CO 42 (42, 46, 48, 50) sts. Work even in St st for 2", ending with a RS row.

Next row: (WS) P21 (21, 23, 24, 25), PM for center of sleeve, P21 (21, 23, 24, 25).

Inc 1 st each end of needle every 4th row 9 (15, 13, 17, 22) times, then every 6th row 7 (3, 5, 3, 0) times (74 [78, 82, 88, 94] sts). At the same time, when sleeve measures 6" (6", 6¾", 7¼", 7") from CO, ending with a WS row, work to 6 sts before marker, PM, work row 1 of chart B, removing center marker, PM at end of chart sts, knit to end of row. Work rows 1–34 of chart 2 times, then work even until piece measures 17½" (17½", 18¼", 18¾", 18½") from CO, ending with a WS row.

Shape cap: BO 4 (4, 5, 6, 8) sts at beg of next 2 rows, then BO 3 (3, 4, 5, 6) sts at beg of foll 2 rows. (60 [64, 64, 66, 66] sts rem.) Dec 1 st each end of needle every RS row 14 (14, 15, 16, 17) times. (32 [36, 34, 34, 32] sts rem.) BO 2 sts at beg of next 4 rows. (24 [28, 26, 26, 24] sts rem.) BO 4 (5, 3, 2, 0) sts at beg of next 2 (2, 2, 2, 0) rows. (16 [18, 20, 22, 24] sts rem.) BO rem sts.

Finishing

Weave in the ends. With RS tog, sew shoulder seams. Sew in sleeves. Sew sleeve and side seams, turning the slip stitch selvedge at the beginning of each row to the inside.

Collar

With MC, RS facing, and 16" circular needle, beg at right shoulder, pick up and knit 54 (54, 62, 68, 76) sts evenly spaced around neck. PM and join for working in the rnd. Work in St st for 2" or desired length. BO all sts loosely. Weave in the ends.

Garment measurements

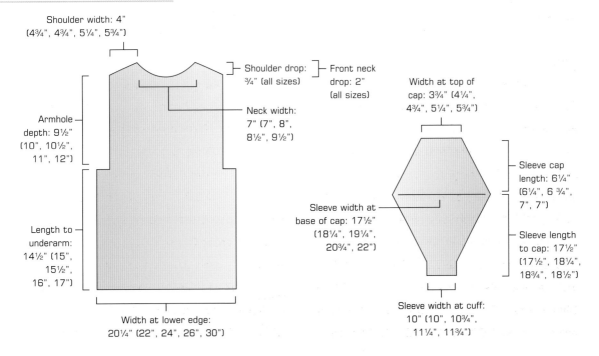

Shoulder width: 4"
(4¾", 4¾", 5¼", 5¾")

Shoulder drop: ¾" (all sizes)

Front neck drop: 2" (all sizes)

Width at top of cap: 3¾" (4¼", 4¾", 5¼", 5¾")

Armhole depth: 9½" (10", 10½", 11", 12")

Neck width: 7" (7", 8", 8½", 9½")

Sleeve cap length: 6¼" (6¼", 6¾", 7", 7")

Length to underarm: 14½" (15", 15½", 16", 17")

Sleeve width at base of cap: 17½" (18¼", 19¼", 20¾", 22")

Sleeve length to cap: 17½" (17½", 18¼", 18¾", 18½")

Width at lower edge: 20¼" (22", 24", 26", 30")

Sleeve width at cuff: 10" (10", 10¾", 11¼", 11¾")

Intarsia

Intarsia—or "picture knitting"—is one of two primary methods of introducing more than one color in a row. Intarsia (versus Fair Isle) is best used for any pattern where more than two colors are needed to create a picture or large asymmetrical blocks of color. Remember always to bring the "old yarn" over the "new yarn" when working intarsia, to avoid holes appearing in your work.

Working from bobbins

When working in intarsia, using the yarn straight from the ball presents a challenge. Bobbins can be purchased at most yarn stores, and are essentially pieces of plastic designed to hold short lengths of yarn—making it easier for you to twist two colors at each juncture. Alternatively, you can measure out a foot or two of yarn and let it hang off the back of the work—unwound.

Before you begin knitting an intarsia chart, wind off enough bobbins for the areas of color you'll be working in. For example, in the Argyle Pullover Vest (see pages 96–100), the green diamond is one complete area of color and is uninterrupted by another color, thus, one bobbin of green should do it. On either side of the diamond there are two areas of red—and the diamond interrupts them. Because you're not planning on carrying the green across the back of the work, it's best to use two bobbins of red.

Chart A

Note: RS rows are worked right to left, WS rows are worked left to right.

Chart B

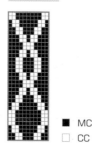

■ MC
□ CC

Twisting the yarn

In intarsia, whenever you switch between two colors, it's imperative that the "old yarn," or the color you're about to stop working with, is twisted over and around the "new yarn," or the color you're about to start working with. This process is relatively easy.

1. On your first row, knit all of the stitches in the first color you're using. To add a new color, insert the right-hand needle into the next stitch, hang a piece of yarn (your new bobbin) off the needle (leaving a 6" tail) and begin working with the new color. Repeat this process for every new bobbin.

2. On the first WS row you'll begin twisting the yarns as you switch colors. Assuming that you're working in stockinette stitch, purl to the end of the first section of color. Then bring the yarn you're about to stop working with (both the yarn and the tail) over and to the left of the color you're about to start working with. Pick up the new color from underneath the old color and begin working with it. Repeat this process, bringing both yarn and tail over the new yarn (on this row only), for every new section of color across the row.

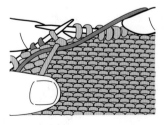

3. On the third row, continue to twist the yarns as you did on the second row (leaving the tail behind), but always bringing the old color over and to the left of the new color. Where more yarn must be added, repeat the process, using these steps as a guide.

Aran Pullover

Among knitters it's pretty well known that when a sailor lost at sea was washed ashore, the unique designs on his sweater led to the identity of the poor soul. Yet what's not well known is that these distinctive Aran garments were often knitted by fishermen themselves—while waiting for work or even for the tides to change. This Aran Pullover, knit with lanolin-rich Shetland wool, features traditional shapes inspired by the sea and makes a perfect complement for sea-faring outfits (or others).

Stitch Guide

Double moss stitch

(Multiples of 4)

Row 1: (RS) *K2 P2, rep from *.

Row 2: *K2 P2, rep from *.

Row 3: *P2 K2, rep from *.

Row 4: *P2 K2, rep from *.

Repeat rows 1–4 for patt.

below The rugged look of an Aran sweater stands out at sea—or on the shore.

Finished measurements: 42" (44½", 48", 52½", 59½") **Yarn:** Jamieson's Shetland Double Knitting 25g (82 yds.); shade: 160 Midnight; 24 (26, 29, 32, 38) balls

Needles: 16" and 24", US size-4 circular needles; 24", US size-5 circular needle

Notions: Tapestry needle; stitch markers

Gauge: 22 sts and 30 rows = 4" in St st on larger needle; little plait cable = 1½"; bulky double cable = 2⅝"; 1 rep of shadow cable = 1⅜"; 20 double moss sts = 4"

To save time and sanity:
TAKE TIME TO CHECK THE GAUGE.

Back

With smaller needle, CO 130 (142, 150, 166, 186) sts. Work in rib as foll: Sl 1 pwise, *K2 P2, rep from * to last st, K1. Rep this row until piece measures 2" from CO, ending with a WS row. Change to larger needle. Knit 1 row, inc 22 (20, 20, 18, 22) sts evenly spaced across (152 [162, 170, 184, 208] sts).

Setup row for cables: (WS) Sl 1 pwise, P0 (0, 0, 2, 0), *K2 P2, rep from * 1 (1, 2, 2, 3) more time(s), K2, PM, K2, P9, K2, PM, P1, K2, P12, K2, P1, PM, K2, P9, K2, PM, P42, (52, 52, 62, 82), PM, K2, P9, K2, PM, P1, K2, P12, K2, P1, PM, K2, P9, K2, PM, P0 (0, 0, 2, 0), *K2,, P2, rep from * 1 (1, 2, 2, 3) more time(s), K3.

Beg main body cable panels, beg with row 1 of each patt: Sl 1 pwise, work 10 (10, 14, 16, 18) sts in double moss st, work 13 sts of little plait cable, work 18 sts of bulky double cable, work 13 sts of little plait cable, work 42 (52, 52, 62, 82) sts in shadow cable, work 13 sts of little plait cable, work 18 sts of bulky double cable, work 13 sts of little plait cable, work 10 (10, 14, 16, 18) sts in double moss st, K1. Cont in patts as established until piece measures 14½" (15", 15", 15", 15") from CO, ending with a WS row.

Shape armholes: BO 10 (10, 8, 14, 14) sts at beg of next 2 rows. (132 [142, 154, 156, 180] sts rem.) Work even until armholes measure 10½" (11", 12", 13", 15"), ending with a WS row. BO all sts.

Front

Work as for back until armholes measure 8" (8½", 9½", 10½", 12½"), ending with a WS row.

Shape neck: With RS facing, work across 56 (56, 56, 57, 65) sts, join a new ball of yarn and BO 20 (30, 42, 42, 50) sts, work to end of row. (56 [56, 56, 57. 65] sts rem each side.)

Right shoulder: Work 1 WS row even. BO 3 sts at neck edge (beg of RS rows) once, then BO 2 sts at neck edge every other row 2 times. (49 [49, 49, 50, 58] sts rem.) Dec 1 st at neck edge every other row 3 times. (46 [46, 46, 47, 55] sts rem.) Work even until armhole measures 10½" (11", 12", 13", 15"). BO rem sts.

Left shoulder: With WS facing, BO 3 sts at neck edge and work to end of row in pattern. (53 [53, 53, 54, 62] sts rem.) BO 2 sts at neck edge (beg of WS rows) 2 times. (49 [49, 49, 50, 58] sts rem.) Dec 1 st at neck edge every other row 3 times. (46 [46, 46, 47, 55] sts rem.) Work even until armhole measures 10½" (11", 12", 13", 15"). BO rem sts.

Sleeves

With smaller needle, CO 62 (62, 66, 66, 70) sts. Working back and forth, work in rib as for body until piece measures 2" from CO, ending with a WS row. Change to larger needle and knit 1 row, inc 8 sts evenly spaced across (70 [70, 74, 74, 78] sts).

Setup for cables: (WS) Sl 1 pwise, K0 (0, 2, 2, 0), *P2 K2, rep from * 2 (2, 2, 2, 3) more times, PM, K2, P9, K2, PM, P1, K2, P12, K2, P1, PM, K2, P9, K2, PM, K0 (0, 2, 2, 0), *P2, K2, rep from * 2 (2, 2, 2, 3) more times, K1.

Work sleeve cables as follows: Sl 1 pwise, work 12 (12, 14, 14, 16) sts in double moss st, work 13 sts of little plait cable, work 18 sts of bulky double cable, work 13 sts of little plait cable, work 12 (12, 14, 14, 16) sts in double moss st, K1. On next RS row, begin increases for sleeve as foll, working new sts in double moss st: K1 M1, work to last st, M1 K1 (2 sts increased). Work 3 (3, 3, 1, 1) row(s) even. Rep these 4 (4, 4, 2, 2) rows 20 (26, 28, 25, 21) more times (112 [124, 132, 86, 122] sts). Inc 1 st each end of needle every 6th (6th, 6th, 4th, 4th) row 6 (2, 3, 31, 23) times (124 [128, 138, 148, 168] sts.) Work even until piece measures 22½" (23", 24", 24½", 24½") from CO. BO all sts.

Little plait cable

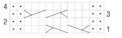

Bulky double cable

Shadow cable

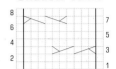

	knit on a RS row, purl on a WS row
	purl on a RS row, knit on a WS row
	slip 3 sts to a cable needle and hold at front, K3, K3 from cable needle
	slip 3 sts to a cable needle and hold at back, K3, K3 from cable needle
	indicates pattern repeat

Finishing

With RS tog, sew shoulder seams. Sew in sleeves. Sew sleeve and side seams (the slip stitch selvedge at the beginning of each row will turn naturally to the inside as you seam).

Garment measurements

Collar

With 16" circular needle and RS facing, pick up and knit 80 (100, 116, 124, 136) sts evenly spaced around neck. PM and join for working in the rnd. Work in K2 P2 rib for 1". BO all sts loosely. Weave in the ends.

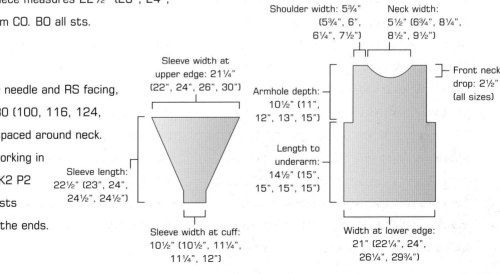

Shoulder width: 5¾" (5¾", 6", 6¼", 7½")

Neck width: 5½" (6¾", 8¼", 8½", 9½")

Front neck drop: 2½" (all sizes)

Armhole depth: 10½" (11", 12", 13", 15")

Length to underarm: 14½" (15", 15", 15", 15")

Width at lower edge: 21" (22¼", 24", 26¼", 29¾")

Sleeve width at upper edge: 21¼" (22", 24", 26", 30")

Sleeve length: 22½" (23", 24", 24½", 24½")

Sleeve width at cuff: 10½" (10½", 11¼", 11¼", 12")

Knee-Length Coat

Aside from dressy outerwear, sweaters and coats rarely travel below the waistline on today's man. But since the dawn of knitted garments, women have benefited from countless knit coat patterns. Here's to equality: using Noro's Iro, a chunky silk/wool blend in a self-striping yarn, the Knee-Length Coat features color and texture while preserving uniquely masculine details such as a shaped lapel, fitted sleeves, and a foldover collar.

> **Tip**
>
> In cases where sweaters or afghans have multiple pieces, it's sometimes helpful to sew as you go, rather than leaving the pieces to the end, to avoid confusing them at that stage.

below This garment provides comfortable, go-anywhere style.

Finished measurements: 43" (52", 61")

Yarn: Noro Iro 100 g (131 yd.); 75% wool, 25% silk; shade: 19; 10 (13, 15) hanks

Needles: 24", US size-11 circular needle

Notions: Tapestry needle; cable needle; five 1½" buttons **Gauge:** 12 sts and 18 rows = 4" in St st

To save time and sanity:
TAKE TIME TO CHECK THE GAUGE.

Left back

Note: Slip first st of each row pwise throughout the garment for ease of finishing.

CO 38 (46, 54) sts. Work even in little front twist pattern until piece measures 26" (28", 29") from CO, ending with a RS row.

Shape armhole: BO 4 (5, 6) sts at armhole edge. Work 1 row even. BO 3 (4, 5) sts at armhole edge. (31 [37, 43] sts rem.) Dec 1 st at armhole edge every RS row 4 (4, 6) times. (27 [33, 37] sts rem.) Work even until armhole measures 9" (11", 12"), ending with a RS row.

Shape shoulder: BO 8 (9, 10) sts at armhole edge. (19 [24, 27] sts rem.) Work 1 row even. BO 7 (9, 10) sts at armhole edge. (12 [15, 17] sts rem.) Work 1 row even. BO rem 12 (15, 17) sts.

Right back

CO 38 (46, 54) sts. Work even in little back twist pattern until piece measures 26" (28", 29") from CO, ending with a WS row.

Shape armhole: BO 4 (5, 6) sts at armhole edge. Work 1 row even. BO 3 (4, 5) sts at armhole edge. (31 [37, 43] sts rem.) Dec 1 st at armhole edge every RS row 4 (4, 6) times. (27 [33, 37] sts rem.) Work even until armhole measures 9" (11", 12"), ending with a WS row.

Shape shoulder: BO 8 (9, 10) sts at armhole edge. (19 [24, 27] sts rem.) Work 1 row even. BO 7 (9, 10) sts at armhole edge. (12 [15, 17] sts rem.) Work 1 row even. BO rem 12 (15, 17) sts. Sew left back and right back together to prepare for finishing, and set aside.

Left front

CO 38 (46, 54) sts. Work even in little back twist pattern until piece measures 26" (28", 29") from CO, ending with a WS row.

Shape armhole: BO 4 (5, 6) sts at armhole edge. Work 1 row even. BO 3 (4, 5) sts at armhole edge. (31 [37, 43] sts rem.) Dec 1 st at beg of each RS row 4 (4, 6) times. (27 [33, 37] sts rem.) Work even until armhole measures 3", ending with a WS row.

Shape neck: Dec 1 st at neck edge every RS row 12 (13, 15) times. (15 [20, 22] sts rem.) Dec 1 st at neck edge every other RS row 0 (2, 2) times. (15 [18, 20] sts rem.) Work even until armhole measures 9" (11", 12"), ending with a WS row.

Shape shoulder: BO 8 (9, 10) sts at armhole edge. (7 [9, 10] sts rem.) Work 1 row even. BO rem 7 (9, 10) sts.

Right front

CO 38 (46, 54) sts. Work even in little front twist pattern until piece measures 26" (28", 29") from CO, ending with a RS row.

Shape armhole: BO 4 (5, 6) sts at armhole edge. Work 1 row even. BO 3 (4, 5) sts at armhole edge. (31 [37, 43] sts rem.) Dec 1 st at armhole edge every RS row 4 (4, 6) times. (27 [33, 37] sts rem.) Work even until armhole measures 3", ending with a RS row.

Shape neck: Dec 1 st at neck edge every RS row 12 (13, 15) times. (15 [20, 22] sts rem.) Dec 1 st at neck edge every other RS row 0 (2, 2) times. (15 [18, 20] sts rem.) Work even until armhole measures 9" (11", 12"), ending with a RS row.

Shape shoulder: BO 8 (9, 10) sts at armhole edge. (7 [9, 10] sts rem.) Work 1 row even. BO rem 7 (9, 10) sts.

Right sleeve

CO 38 (46, 46) sts. Work even in little back twist pattern until piece measures 2½" from CO, ending with a RS row. Inc 1 st each end of needle every 4th row 15 (15, 18) times, working new sts into pattern (68 [76, 82] sts). Work even until piece measures 17" (18¾", 18½") from CO, ending with a WS row.

Shape cap: BO 5 (5, 6) sts at beg of next 2 rows. (58 [66, 70] sts rem.) BO 4 (4, 5) sts at beg of foll 2 rows. (50 [58, 60] sts rem.) Dec 1 st at each end of needle every RS row 9 (11, 14) times. (32 [36, 32] sts rem.) BO 3 sts at beg of next 2 rows. (26 [30, 26] sts rem.) BO 5 (6, 3) sts at beg of foll 2 rows. (16 [18, 20] sts rem.) BO rem 16 (18, 20) sts.

Left sleeve

Work as for right sleeve, working little front twist pattern instead of little back twist pattern.

Finishing

Sew the shoulder seams. Sew sleeves to armholes. Sew sleeve and side seams. Weave in all the ends.

Button band

CO 6 sts. Work in K1 P1 rib until piece measures 28" (30", 31") from CO, ending with a RS row. Cont in rib, inc 1 st at beg of every WS row 14 times, as foll:

Row 1: (WS) Kfb P1 *K1 P1, rep from *.

Row 2: *K1 P1, rep from * to last st, K1.

Row 3: Kfb *K1 P1, rep from *.

Row 4: *K1 P1, rep from *.

Rep rows 1–4 six more times (20 sts). Work even in rib until piece measures 35" (39", 41") from CO, ending with a WS row. BO all sts. Sew button band to right front. Beg 8" from bottom of button band, sew buttons to band, placing them every 5" (5½", 5¾"), placing last button 28" (30", 31") from CO.

Buttonhole band

CO 6 sts. Work in K1 P1 rib until piece measures 8", ending with a WS row. On next RS row, make buttonhole as follows: K1 P1, yo twice, SSK, work in patt to end of row. On next row, drop second yo from needle. (Do not work into second yo.) Cont in patt, making a buttonhole as above every 5" (5½", 5¾"), until piece measures 28" (30", 31") from CO, ending with a WS row (5 buttonholes). Cont in rib, inc 1 st at beg of every RS row 14 times, as foll:

Row 1: (RS) Kfb P1 *K1 P1, rep from *.

Row 2: *K1 P1, rep from * to last st, K1.

Row 3: Kfb *K1 P1, rep from *.

Row 4: *K1 P1, rep from *.

Rep rows 1–4 six more times (20 sts). Work even in rib until piece measures 35" (39", 41") from CO, ending with a WS row. BO all sts. Sew buttonhole band to left front.

Collar

With RS facing, beg at right shoulder, pick up and knit 24 (30, 32) sts across back to left shoulder. Work in K1 P1 rib, inc 1 st each end of needle every RS row and working new sts into rib, until piece measures 2½" from CO, ending with a WS row. BO all sts loosely. Weave in ends. Tack 1" at bottom side of collar to the top of each band so that join rests just below the shoulder seam..

Little front twist

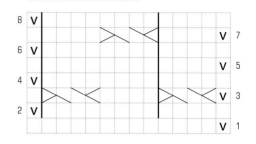

Little back twist

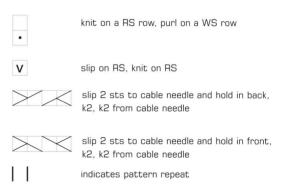

Note: RS rows are worked right to left, WS rows are worked left to right.

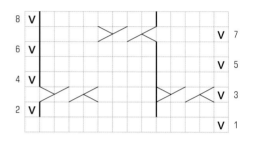

	knit on a RS row, purl on a WS row
	slip on RS, knit on RS
	slip 2 sts to cable needle and hold in back, k2, k2 from cable needle
	slip 2 sts to cable needle and hold in front, k2, k2 from cable needle
	indicates pattern repeat

Garment measurements

Front

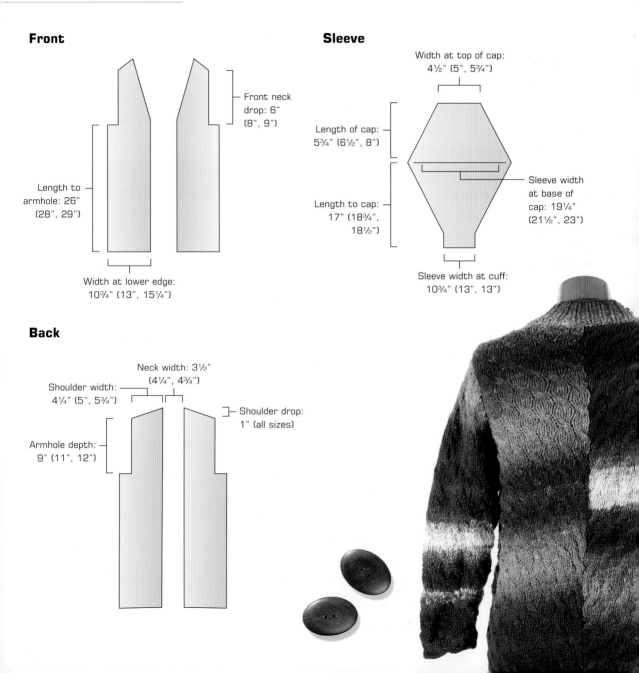

Front neck
drop: 6"
(8", 9")

Length to
armhole: 26"
(28", 29")

Width at lower edge:
10¾" (13", 15¼")

Sleeve

Width at top of cap:
4½" (5", 5¾")

Length of cap:
5¾" (6½", 8")

Length to cap:
17" (18¾",
18½")

Sleeve width
at base of
cap: 19¼"
(21½", 23")

Sleeve width at cuff:
10¾" (13", 13")

Back

Neck width: 3½"
(4¼", 4¾")

Shoulder width:
4¼" (5", 5¾")

Shoulder drop:
1" (all sizes)

Armhole depth:
9" (11", 12")

The basics of finishing

When you spend so many hours working to make a garment that you'd like to last, it really is worth taking the extra time to be sure that the seams and finishing touches look good—despite the fact that you're so eager to use it!

Adding a new ball of yarn

1. With the ball of yarn you're about to start working with, make a slip knot.

2. Thread the tail of the finished ball through the slip knot and pull it tight, moving the slip knot so that it rests close to the knitted work.

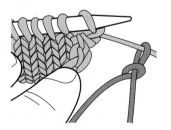

3. Begin knitting with the new yarn, leaving both tails to be sewn in later.

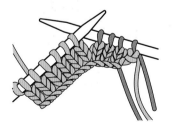

It's best to add yarns at the beginning of a RS or WS row whenever possible, always remembering to leave enough yarn to weave in later.

Weaving in the ends

Under the finishing section in nearly all garments, a pattern will tell the reader to weave in the ends. Here, the main objective is to secure your ends in place so that the edges don't unravel. When you're ready to weave in your ends, follow the steps below as a guide—being sure not to introduce any bulkiness where you weave, which may affect the look or texture of the finished garment. Note that ends often come "unwoven" when seaming pieces of a garment together, so in the case of a sweater or vest, delay weaving in your ends until all the pieces have been sewn together.

> **Tip**
>
> When weaving in ends, you may also want to weave in a few extra feet of left-over yarn around the seams. Later, if the seams break or a button falls loose, you'll know exactly where to find extra yarn.

1. Begin by threading an end that needs to be woven in onto a tapestry needle. Then insert the tip of the needle through a stitch on the WS of the work, pulling the yarn through.

2. Now insert the tip of the needle into the same stitch, in the same direction as in step 1, and pull through. Repeat this process across three or four stitches, keeping the tails woven in on the edges of the piece.

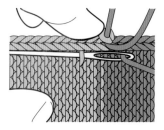

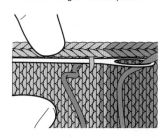

Resist the temptation to leave big knots, which can create unsightly bumps or bulges, and spoil the end result!

Selvedge stitches

In selvedge stitches (also known as slipped stitches or seam allowances), the first stitch of every row is slipped knitwise or purlwise. While not entirely necessary on many garments, it makes finishing significantly easier, because it is clear where the pieces should be sewn together and how they should lie—based on the indication of the stitches.

To slip a stitch knitwise

1. Insert the tip of the right-hand needle into the stitch as if to knit, but don't wrap the yarn around the needle.

2. Pull the stitch off the left-hand needle onto the right needle, leaving it unworked. When complete, a knitwise selvedge stitch resembles a noticeably raised bump at the beginning of the row.

> **Tip**
>
> In addition to easing finishing, selvedge stitches can be added to the edge of a scarf, shawl, or throw to give the item a finished edge or to reduce curling on the edges.

To slip a stitch purlwise

1. Insert the tip of the right-hand needle into the stitch as if to purl, but don't wrap the yarn around the needle.

2. Pull the stitch off the left-hand needle onto the right-hand needle, leaving it unworked. When complete, a purlwise selvedge stitch resembles an open V-shape, similar to a knit stitch in stockinette fabric.

Three-needle bindoff

The three-needle bindoff is often used to join two pieces of fabric where lengths of live stitches have been put on holders (often seen in shoulders or hoods). While the technique creates an almost invisible seam, edges that have been bound off and sewn together actually create a stronger join. When working a three-needle bindoff, it's always best to start at the outermost part of the seam (i.e. the forehead of the hood, or the outermost part of the shoulder) and work your way inward.

1. Arrange the stitches on two needles, so that half of the total number of stitches rest on one needle and the other half rest on the other needle. The RS of the work should be facing inward and both needle ends should be facing in the same direction.

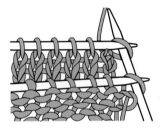

2. Insert a third needle of the same size into the first stitch on both needles—as though you're knitting together the first stitch from the needle in front and the first stitch from the needle in back. Wrap the yarn around the needle and pull it out of both stitches, then slide both off the needle together. There should be one loop on the right-hand needle.

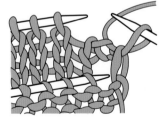

3. Repeat the process from the beginning of step 2. There are now two stitches on the left-hand needle. Proceed to BO one stitch, using the traditional method.

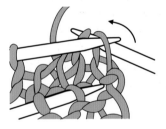

4. Repeat the process from step 2 for each set of stitches on the left-hand needles, then BO one stitch of the resulting two on the right-hand needle, across the row. When the last stitch has been bound off, end the piece as you would with a traditional bindoff.

Joining two boundoff seams

Often two boundoff edges are sewn to one another—as in the case of two shoulders. This is a fairly simple process because the edges are easily recognized. As with joining any pieces, be careful not to pull too tightly.

1. Line up the two edges to be sewn together, with the boundoff stitches topside and the RS facing. The boundoff stitches should be even and in line with one another.

2. With yarn threaded on a tapestry needle, insert the needle from front to back under both sets of loops from the boundoff stitches and pull through. Then, working from back to front, repeat the process, inserting the needle under both sets of loops and pulling it through.

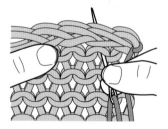

Joining boundoff to selvedge

When a sleeve must be eased into an armhole, a boundoff edge will be joined to a selvedge. But take care! The ratio of selvedge stitches and boundoff stitches isn't always equal, and some fudging will need to be done, as described here.

1. Begin by pinning the boundoff edge to the selvedge stitches with the RS facing. With yarn threaded on a tapestry needle, starting at the shoulder and moving your way down to the underarm, insert the needle from back to front at the shoulder seam.

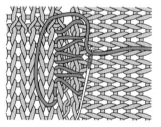

2. Insert the tapestry needle under two bars from the sleeve and two bars from the shoulder, and pull through. Over the next three stitches, insert the tapestry needle under one bar from the sleeve and two bars from the shoulder. Repeat these four movements down to the underarm and the same down the other side.

Joining selvedge to selvedge

Selvedge stitches, though sometimes difficult to remember to work on each row, make for a spectacular finish to seaming a garment. Once the stitched pieces are lined up, recognizing where to stick the needle is easy as pie.

1. Line up the two pieces of fabric to be sewn together, and pin them together using safety pins, with RS facing. Then, starting at the first stitch on the right piece, insert the needle under one stitch on the right-hand piece and one stitch on the left-hand piece. Pull the yarn through. Repeat this process all the way up the garment.

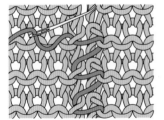

Knitted cast-on

A midrow cast-on (also known as the "knit-on" method) is ideal for any situation where you need to add additional stitches to a garment in the middle or at the end of a row.

1. Make a slip knot and place it on the left-hand needle in the same way you would if you were beginning a cable cast-on. Insert the needle as if to knit this stitch.

2. Pull the loop out of the stitch and insert it directly back onto the needle. Knit this new stitch, pulling a loop out and inserting the stitch onto the left-hand needle. Repeat this process for the number of stitches that must be cast on.

Whipstitch

A whipstitch—a simple way of joining two knitted pieces—is perfect for situations where the seam becomes a design element of the finished item.

1. Insert the needle from back to front on the piece, bringing the needle and yarn through both pieces of fabric, and pull the yarn through, leaving a 6" tail.

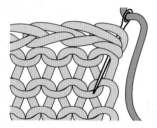

2. Reinsert the needle just above the place where you inserted it in step 1, wrapping the yarn around the seam where the two pieces of fabric meet, and pull the needle through.

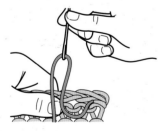

Repeat step 2 all the way across the seam, and then weave in the end.

Home Gear

Dog Tooth Throw

The dog tooth pattern—or a series of broken checks forming four pointed stars—is a standard when it comes to fabric for men's clothing, resting right up there with plaid among masculine motifs. Knit in individual squares using Nashua's Creative Focus Worsted, and then pieced to form the design, the Dog Tooth Throw is great for any guy looking to add a bit of warmth to his couch or bed, without sacrificing personal style.

> **Tip**
>
> At first glance, a blanket composed of 24 panels sewn together might seem a bit of a burden. But at just 9" a piece, this makes for great travel knitting.

below A great masculine motif for the home.

Finished measurements: 40" x 58" (with border) **Yarn:** Nashua Creative Focus Worsted (220 yd.); 75% wool, 25% alpaca; shade: 1660 Marine, 3 balls (MC1); shade: 0401 Nickel, 3 balls (MC2); shade: 0500 Ebony, 2 balls (CC1) **Needles:** 48" US size-8 straight needles; 48" US-size 8 circular needle **Notions:** Tapestry needle **Gauge:** 18 sts and 26 rows = 4" in St st

To save time and sanity:
TAKE TIME TO CHECK THE GAUGE.

Panels

With MC1, CO 43 sts. Work in St st until piece measures 4.5" from CO, ending on a WS row. Next row, change to MC2. Work in St st until piece measures 9" from CO. BO all sts. Make 23 more panels to match.

Finishing

Arrange the panels to match the Dog Tooth Throw Chart. With CC1 and WS facing, whipstitch the panels together in columns of 6. Then whipstitch the columns together to form the full throw. Weave in all ends.

Dog Tooth Throw Chart

Border

With CC1 and a 48", US size-8 circular needle, at one long edge pick up and knit 220 sts. Knit in garter stitch for 2". BO all sts loosely. Rep on the other long edge.

At one short edge, pick up and knit 175 sts, including sts from garter st edges from the long edge borders. Knit in garter st for 2". BO all sts loosely. Rep on the other short edge. Weave in the rem ends.

Tip

When casting on (or picking up) a huge number of stitches, placing a marker every 25 stitches or so will make it easier for you to count the total number of stitches when you're ready to start working.

Beer Cozy

Since the dawn of time, man has struggled against all odds to keep beer cold. Once the heavenly brew is pulled from the cooler, a chain of events is set into motion that can only end in warm beer and hands dripping with condensation. Slip this cozy on, however, and you're good to go! Made with a stretchy blend of cotton and Lycra, the beer cozy provides modest shade from the sun—and means no more coasters.

below Perfect in winter, too, when your fingers are cold!

Finished measurements (to fit any ordinary beer bottle): 7.75" around, 5.5" tall, 2" diameter at bottom of cozy **Yarn:** Cascade Fixation (100 yd. relaxed); 98.3% cotton, 1.7% elastic; shade: 3794 (shown left with 7360 and 5606); 1 ball **Needles:** set of 4 US size-6 double-pointed needles **Notions:** stitch marker; tapestry needle **Gauge:** 22 sts and 40 rows = 4" in St st, worked in the rnd

To save time and sanity:
TAKE TIME TO CHECK THE GAUGE.

Pattern

CO 6 sts. Divide sts evenly among 3 double-pointed needles and join, being careful not to twist sts. Place marker (PM).

Rnd 1: Knit.

Rnd 2: *K1 yo repeat from * to end of rnd (12 sts).

Rnd 3 (and all odd rnds): Knit.

Rnd 4: *K2 yo repeat from * to end of rnd (18 sts).

Rnd 6: *K3 yo repeat from * to end of rnd (24 sts).

Rnd 8: *K4 yo repeat from * to end of rnd (30 sts).

Rnd 10: *K5 yo repeat from * to end of rnd (36 sts).

Work in St st until piece measures 2" from start. Beg rnd 1 of any one of the pattern stitches above and work for 3". Beg next row: work reverse St st for 1". BO all stitches very loosely.

Finishing

Sew in ends and block, if necessary, by wetting the cozy, then sliding it over the beer bottle to dry.

> **Tip**
>
> When working on double-pointed needles, try to position your purl stitches at the end of the needle. It's far easier (and a heck of a lot neater) to start on fresh knit stitches after working some purls, than vice versa.

3 x 3 rib

woven rib

3 cross cable

Stitch Guide

3 x 3 rib

(in the rnd)

(Multiples of 3)

Rnd 1: *K3 P3 repeat from *.

Repeat rnd 1 for patt.

Stitch Guide

Reverse

stockinette stitch

(in the rnd)

Rnd 1: Purl.

Repeat rnd 1 for patt.

Stitch Guide

Woven rib

(Multiples of 6)

Rnd 1–8: *K3 P3 repeat from *.

Rnd 9, 10: Knit.

Rnd 11–18: *P3 K3 repeat

from *.

Rnd 19–20: Knit.

Work rnds 1–20 for patt.

Stitch Guide

3 cross cable

(Multiples of 9)

Rnds 1, 2: *K6 P3 repeat from *.

Rnd 3: *(Slip 3 sts to a cable

needle and hold at front of

work, K3, K3 sts from cable

needle) P3 repeat from *.

Rnds 4–7: *K6 P3 repeat from *.

Repeat rnds 1–7 for pattern.

Felted Travel Bag

Beyond holding our precious travel commodities—toothpaste, toothbrush, shaving soap, and a razor—the travel bag does its best to protect the rest of our luggage from accidental spills. But that doesn't mean we need to carry around those drab, flimsy black things they sell in department stores—or, in true bachelor fashion, rely on an extra plastic bag. The Felted Travel Bag offers everything we've come to rely on from a commercial travel bag, and is the answer to those stylin' prayers.

> **Tip**
>
> Don't be afraid to get creative when searching out notions and linings. You might find even the ripstock nylon and waterproofing sealant at an outdoor supply store.

below A stylish solution to a travel necessity.

Finished measurements: 10" x 4.75" x 5.5"

Yarn: Manos del Uruguay (138 yd.); 100% wool; shade 104: 2 skeins (MC); shade 40: 1 skein (CC) **Needles:** 26", US size-11 circular needles; set of 5 US size-11 double-pointed needles

Notions: about 1 yd. of 1.9-oz coated waterproof ripstock nylon; small container of waterproofing sealant; polyester sewing thread; piece of quilter's template plastic, cut into a rectangle approximately 10" x 4.75"; tapestry needle; stitch markers; 10" brass zipper; about 2 yd. dental floss (unwaxed); several pieces of plywood, cardboard, or hard plastic for blocking **Gauge:** 13 sts and 16 rows = 4" in St st (prefelt)

To save time and sanity:

TAKE TIME TO CHECK THE GAUGE.

Bag

Note: The first stitch of every row is slipped purlwise. With a circular needle and MC, CO 78 sts. Purl 1 row.

Row 1: Sl 1 pwise K8, P2, PM, K18, P2, PM, K16, P2, PM, K18, P2, PM, K9.

Row 2: Slip 1 pwise P8, K2, P18, K2, P16, K2, P18, K2, P9.

Rep rows 1 and 2 until piece measures 3", ending on a WS row. Cont to work as set, changing colors according to the foll stripe sequence: 1.5" CC, 6" MC, 1.5" CC; always switch colors at beg of a RS row. Switch to MC and cont to work as set until piece measures 15" from start. BO all stitches and weave in the ends.

Thread dental floss onto a tapestry needle and, with the WS facing, sew selvedge stitches from both sides of the piece together to form a long tube. Make sure the ends are secured and the seam is tight.

Turn the tube inside out, so that the RS is facing out.

With double-pointed needles and CC, starting at the left edge of the seam, pick up and knit 9 sts on the WS of the work, using the K2 line as a guide for the edge of the side. Cont down the inside of the work, and on the second double-pointed needle pick up and knit 18 sts. Working across the bottom of the bag and with a third double-pointed needle, pick up and knit 18 sts. With the fourth double-pointed needle, pick up and knit 18 sts. Working now with the other end of the first double-pointed needle, pick up and knit 9 sts on the other side of the seam, placing a marker after the first stitch you pick up (to note the beg of the rnd) (72 sts total). Knit 1 rnd.

Decrease for end

Row 1: Knit to 3 before end of needle 1. K2togtbl K1. Knit to 3 before end of needle 2. K2togtbl K1. Cont in this fashion on needles 3 and 4 (4 sts dec).

Row 2: Knit.

Rep rows 1 and 2 (4) more times (52 sts rem), and then just row 1 (12) more times. (4 sts rem). Thread yarn onto a tapestry needle and pull through the remaining stitches.

Rep stitch pickup and dec for the other end. Weave in all ends.

Strap

With MC, CO 12 sts. Still slipping the first st of every row pwise, knit in St st until piece measures 12.5". BO sts and weave in the ends. Do not attach to the bag.

Finishing

Felt the bag in hot water in your washing machine until the fibers lock (see page 37 for instructions on how to felt). When complete, the bag should be approximately 10" long and the two ends of the bag should lie flat. Once the bag and strap are completely felted, take them out of your washing machine and run them under cold water. Roll the bag and strap up in a towel to squeeze out any remaining water.

Bringing your bag to a flat workspace, cut away the dental floss to open the bag. Using several pieces of cardboard, plywood, or hard plastic, insert the blocking material onto each of the sides in order to set the shape of the bag (CD jewel cases work great on shaping the ends). The strap should dry flat. Allow both pieces to dry for at least 24 hours.

When both pieces are completely dry, remove your blocking materials. Set the piece of quilter's template across the bottom of the bag and baste it in place, sewing the four corners to the bottom of the bag. Then cut the ripstock nylon into two 5.5" x 4.75" pieces of fabric, and one 19.5" x 10" piece of fabric. Using the polyester sewing thread, hand sew the large piece in place, sewing along the edges of the fabric and securing it at the corners of the bag.

Then hand sew the two remaining pieces to the ends of the bag, sewing around the edges of the fabric. Run the waterproofing sealant over the stitches to lock any potential moisture out. Hand sew the zipper to the top seam, and sew the strap to one end of the bag.

Utility Cloth

It's a little-known fact that men wash their faces. In fact, they scrub dishes, wash their cars, and in the end even dust occasionally. Now imagine a cloth that could do all this and more! The Utility Cloth takes the idea of the traditional knitted washcloth and brings it to a whole new level. Worked in a variety of stitch patterns, with the option of several sizes, it's good for just about anything you can throw at it—and, better still, it's machine-washable.

below Three versions of a utility cloth with a difference.

Finished measurements: 9 x 9" (12 x 12", 18 x 12") **Yarn:** Butterfly Super 10 Mercerized Cotton 125 g (253 yd.); shades: 3606 Peridot, 3945 Winter Night, 3567 Gold Leaf; 1 skein per cloth (Note: depending on the size, 1 skein may make more than one washcloth.) **Needles:** US size-7 straight needles **Notions:** Tapestry needle; stitch markers **Gauge:** 16 sts and 30 rows = 4" in St st; 22 sts and 32 rows = 4" in ribbed check; 22 sts and 28 rows = 4" in basketweave; 18 sts and 30 rows = 4" in square seed lattice

To save time and sanity:
TAKE TIME TO CHECK THE GAUGE.

Version 1 pattern

CO 25 (36, 50) sts. Knit 4 (6, 6) rows garter stitch. Maintaining a 2-st (3-st, 3-st) garter border on both ends of the utility cloth, work square seed lattice pattern until piece measures 9" (12", 12"). Knit 4 (6, 6) rows garter stitch. BO all sts loosely. Weave in the ends.

Stitch Guide

Square seed lattice (Multiples of 14 plus 2)

Row 1: (RS) Knit.

Row 2: P2 *(K1 P1) twice, K1 P2 repeat from *.

Row 3: K3 *P1 K1 P1 K4 repeat from * to end last repeat K3.

Row 4: P2 *(K1 P1) twice, K1 P2 repeat from *.

Row 5: K3 *P1 K1 P1 K4 repeat from * to end last repeat K3.

Row 6: P2 *(K1 P1) twice, K1 P2 repeat from *.

Row 7: K3 *P1 K1 P1 K4 repeat from * to end last repeat K3.

Row 8: P2 *K12 P2 repeat from *.

Row 9: K2 *P12 K2 repeat from *.

Row 10: Purl.

Row 11: K2 *(P1 K1) twice, P1 K2 repeat from *.

Row 12: P3 *K1 P1 K1 P4 repeat from * to end last repeat P3.

Row 13: K2 *(P1 K1) twice, P1 K2 repeat from *.

Row 14: P3 *K1 P1 K1 P4 repeat from * to end last repeat P3.

Row 15: K2 *(P1 K1) twice, P1 K2 repeat from *.

Row 16: P3 *K1 P1 K1 P4 repeat from * to end last repeat P3.

Row 17: P7 *K2 P12 repeat from * to end K2 P7.

Row 18: K7 *P2 K12 repeat from * to end P2 K7.

Repeat rows 1–18 for patt.

Version 2 pattern

CO 48 (60, 96) sts. Knit 4 (6, 8) rows garter stitch. Maintaining a 2-st (3-st, 4-st) garter border on both ends of the utility cloth, work ribbed check until piece measures 9" (12", 12"). Knit 4 (6, 8) rows garter stitch. BO all sts loosely. Weave in the ends.

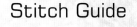

Stitch Guide

Ribbed check

(Even number of sts)

Row 1: *K1 P1 repeat from *.

Row 2: *K1 P1 repeat from *.

Row 3: *P1 K1 repeat from *.

Row 4: *P1 K1 repeat from *.

Repeat rows 1–4 for patt.

Version 1

Version 2

Version 3

Version 3 pattern

CO 48 (64, 96) sts. Beg row 1 of basketweave pattern and work until piece measures 9" (12", 12"). BO all sts loosely. Weave in the ends.

Stitch Guide

Basketweave

(Multiples of 16)

Row 1: *K8 P8 repeat from *.

Rows 2–8: Repeat row 1.

Row 9: *P8 K8 repeat from *.

Rows 10–16: Repeat row 9.

Repeat rows 1–16 for patt.

Tip

A wash cloth is a great way to try out a new stitch pattern or test a new technique. Flip through a stitch dictionary, cast on stitches for a pattern you like using a machine-washable cotton, and give something new a try!

Customizing Patterns & Knitting Resources

Altering patterns

Altering patterns can be a tricky business. On one level, altering a design made for one sex to fit another is as simple as changing a few measurements and altering some obvious shaping. On another, it can be tough to figure out what you really want, and how a different texture or color might significantly change the overall look and style.

The tips and examples in this section explore all these concepts and more, and come from multiple sources (review the Selected Bibliography on page 157 to see some of them), but are mainly from hands-on experience. Though these few pages aren't nearly enough space to fully cover the topic, it's important to note that the most proven method of success in alteration is good planning—and trial and error. The very roots of garment design have always been: *Got an idea? Swatch it up! It works? Great! It doesn't? Try again!*

Getting started

Begin by finding the pattern you'd like to make, but need to alter. Read it through a few times, looking at the photo of the finished item (if there is one) and, using what you already know about garment construction, examine the clues and begin to make some assumptions about what the designer intended in the finished garment:

> **Tip**
>
> A great way to track your design successes and woes is to keep a knitting journal. Something as simple as a ruled notepad will allow you to track pattern notes and changes—as well as yarn information and more.

■ How is the garment constructed? Is it worked in pieces or done in one piece? Is there shaping on the body? On the arms? In the yoke? Is this shaping necessary for your body type or finished look?

■ Are measurements already included for your sizing? Are the sleeves long enough? Do you think you might like to shorten or lengthen the body? The collar?

■ Do you like the stitch pattern? How do you feel about the color? The yarn and fibers? The needle size?

Asking yourself questions like these, make notes directly on the pattern about your first impressions of the garment. Working in pencil, delete any shaping that seems to be incongruent—such as an hourglass shaping (where stitches are cast on for the body, then decreased to give a fitted waistline, and increased to accommodate the bust), or tapered or bell-shaped cuffs on the sleeves. Think about what you like and what you don't—and ultimately what you want to change. Reduce the pattern to its most basic shapes, then rewrite it in your knitting journal, this time in pen.

Next, redraw the schematic included with the pattern (if applicable), removing any shaping that you may have altered, and without any of the numbers. Using the schematic measurements in tandem with a sweater or other garment that you are already familiar with (as Elizabeth Zimmermann suggests in her books), measure and record all the relevant numbers (armhole depth, shoulder width, chest measurement, etc.), and add them to the schematic.

Finally, you may find it helpful to expand your thinking about this new version of the pattern. Try making a sketch and writing a few sentences showing where might they wear it and how might they use it?

Inspiration

As you're making changes to the pattern (described in the previous section), you've probably already got some idea about how you'd like the finished garment to look. But inspiration doesn't stop there: you still need to think about yarn choices, stitch patterns, color, and even length. This can certainly be a challenge, but begin by trusting your instincts—and then challenging them. Don't be afraid to break some sacred rule of garment construction: sometimes the wackiest ideas can lead to profound designs. Also, keep your eyes open. Everything around you can lead to a new idea or concept. Above all, give yourself plenty of time to think about what you'd ultimately like in the new garment. Inspiration rarely flushes itself out overnight—you may even find yourself changing your mind once the needles are in your hands!

Stitch consideration

A staple in any knitter's library is the stitch dictionary. From the invaluable Barbara Walker's *Treasury* to *The Knitter's Bible* and others, a stitch dictionary catalogs the millions of stitches in a knitter's repertoire. With pictures of the finished design and thorough instructions on how to recreate the look, it gives you options you didn't even know you had.

When I'm searching for a stitch, I'll take a pad of sticky notes and a stitch dictionary, and start marking pages with stitches I like. When considering stitches, be sure to weigh all the factors: the finished look, the firmness or looseness of the resulting fabric, and how much work you'll have to do to get the stitch to look the way you want.

Before heading off to your local yarn store, make a list of any notions that you'll need to complete the stitches. Take your notes and pattern with you, to ask the clerk about any techniques you're unsure of and to consider stitch choice in relation to fiber.

Yarn choice and color

As you prepare to enter a yarn store, above all remember this: rely on what you know—and don't be afraid to ask about what you don't know. With a few projects under your belt, you probably have a pretty good idea of what yarns you like working with. Start selecting fibers, colors, and balls of yarn that catch your eye, and momentarily ignore price tags, yardage, gauge, and so on. Evaluate each yarn on its feasibility for the finished product: think about fiber content—angora might look nice, but perhaps it sheds too much for your taste; weight—do you really want to knit a coat in a fingering weight yarn?; and price—can you afford that much cashmere?

Once you've found a yarn you like, think about colorways. Keep in mind that some colors look slightly different in sunlight than they do in indoor lighting; for true color, take your ball of yarn over to the window. Try mixing colors: put two shades that you envision lying next to one another in the garment side by side, then gently pull a strand of each from the ball and twist them.

When you've decided on yarn and color, be sure to buy enough yarn for your garment—from the same dye lot. Compare what the pattern says with the changes you'll be making, and how much yarn your stitch pattern eats up. Then buy an extra ball or two: too much yarn is always better than too little. If you're still unsure, ask the clerk. Make sure you have the right needles for the yarns you're buying, and keep your receipts (exchanging yarns is almost always an option).

Making your swatches

A swatch is a small piece of knitted fabric. Using a specific yarn and stitch pattern, it's a reliable sample of how the knitted fabric will look in your finished garment. Making a swatch is essential in determining the correct fit for a garment, and becomes ultra-important when altering a pattern or writing your own. Whether you're simply changing the type of yarn or the fiber, swatching is vital—if only to get the same number of stitches per inch as the pattern is indicating.

Begin by doing a quick 4" x 4" square in stockinette stitch. This first swatch can tell you a lot about the yarn: how it feels in your fingers, whether it will lie too loosely on the needles you've chosen; and serves as a starting point for your design. Then, looking back at the stitches you've marked in your stitch dictionaries, work one stitch pattern per swatch. Using the number of stitches per inch from the stockinette stitch swatch, cast on enough stitches for a 4" x 4" square (or larger, if you prefer) swatch in that stitch, keeping in mind that any techniques in the stitch pattern (such as cables, lace, or others) can alter the gauge and stretch of the finished fabric. If your garment is knitted in the round, be sure to cast on for working in the round. If it is worked in Fair Isle, make your swatch using the same charts you'll use in the body of the item.

After the first few rows or pattern repeats examine the fabric. Is it too tight or loose? Do you need to change the needle size? Is it already evident this won't meet your needs? Decide either to complete the swatch or to start another—then continue through your chosen stitches.

Once your swatches are complete, wash them according to the instructions on the yarn band and let them dry. Then, when you go to measure your gauge for each, you will be working with the final fabric.

Looking at all your swatches, choose which ones best fit your concept and set the rest aside for use on another project. Then measure the number of stitches and rows per inch for each stitch pattern, and record this information with the rest of your notes. Measuring gauge is extremely important—it will form the basis for all pattern numbers from here on out.

For a review of the principles of gauge, see page 25.

Kitchen math

Determining the cast on number

Working with just your gauge measurements and your schematic, calculate the cast-on number by multiplying the sweater width (or circumference, if you're working in the round) by the number of stitches per inch of the stitch that you're using for the body. So if you're working in seed stitch and you've got 5 stitches to the inch, your total chest measurement is 41", and you're working the body in two equal-sized pieces of 20½" each (the front and the back), you need to multiply:

20½" x 5 sts = 102½ sts

Round this number up or down, to fit the total number of stitches required for your pattern—in this case, seed stitch is worked over multiples of two, so round down to 102. Before finalizing the number, you may choose to add a selvedge (a slipped stitch at the beginning of each row, see page 120) to each side of the sweater to ease the finishing:

102 pattern sts + 2 selvedge sts = 104 sts

Thus, for the front (and back) of your sweater, you'll cast on 104 stitches.

Rewriting the pattern

Rather than casting on right away, you can choose to rewrite the rest of your pattern: sleeves, collar, and all. Working from your notes, record all the relevant details from top to bottom: yarn name; yardage; number of balls; needle size; anticipated notions; gauge; and finally, pattern instructions. Using the measurements on your schematic, gauge measurements, and pattern as a guide, rewrite: the number of stitches to cast on; how long to work the body before the armholes; how to shape the armholes; and how to work the shoulders and bind off; how to cast on for the sleeves; how to shape the sleeves; and how the garment is constructed.

Shaping tips and tricks

In some situations you'll be unable to determine the shaping of an armhole or a sleeve because a pattern schematic won't give you all the relevant details. However, all is not lost! Say the pattern doesn't state how wide the sleeve cuff is, but you know the gauge in the pattern is 4 sts per inch, and that 32 sts are cast on for the sleeve.

Assuming that the gauge of the yarn you're using is 6 sts per inch, you would determine the width of the sleeve cuff as:

Total number of stitches given **divided by** stitches per inch (as it's written in the original pattern) = Sleeve Width.

So, in this case, *32 sts ÷ 4 sts per inch = 8"*

To get the number of stitches you'll need to cast on, using the yarn that gives you 6 sts per inch, multiply:

Total width of sleeve cuff (per above) **by** the number of stitches per inch in your yarn = the number of stitches to cast on.

So, *8" x 6 sts per inch = 48 sts*

This technique can be used in all sorts of situations where measurements aren't provided and you'll need to ensure a good fit—such as armhole shaping at the body, front collar width, or shoulder width. When using gauge to determine measurements that aren't provided, bear in mind that this works best with the sizes stated by the pattern. If you're working in a size much larger (or smaller) than the pattern gives, you may need to fudge the numbers a bit—or go back to your favorite sweater and take the measurement from there to use as a guide. Remember always to take into account that different stitches provide different gauges, and that when determining numbers for a cast-on (or boundoff edge), the width of the item should be multiplied by the total number of stitches per inch in the pattern you're using. Finally, take stitch multiples into account; make sure that if your stitch is a multiple of 6 plus 2, then your cast-on edge is a multiple of 6 plus 2—not counting any additional selvedge stitches.

Sleeve increases

Another issue is determining increases for a sleeve. If, looking at your pattern, it says: "Once cuff is complete, increase 1 stitch each end of row, every 8th row, 10 times. Work even until piece measures 18" from cuff," then, looking back at the gauge information provided at the start of the pattern, you know that 32 rows = 4" or 8 rows = 1", so in this case they're increasing 2 sts every inch of fabric. Working with these numbers, turn your attention to your pattern and yarn. Your row gauge, in the pattern stitch you're working the sleeves in, is 40 rows = 4" or 10 rows = 1". Working off the pattern as a template, you'll also be increasing 2 sts every inch of fabric, so your pattern instruction will read something like: "Once cuff is complete, increase 1 stitch each end of row, every 10th row, 10 times. Work even until piece measures 18" from cuff." When using this method to determine sleeve increases, make sure that your sleeve cap width is the same measurement as the pattern schematic is telling you it should be, using the technique described on the previous page.

Knitting the garment

Now that you've done the math, you've got a pretty good idea of how things will look and you've got a pattern to work with. Get ready to move through the steps as you've outlined them. Rip back if it seems you should—and occasionally charge forward when you feel you should stop. Keep excellent notes throughout: mark down what worked and what didn't. Never rely on what the pattern tells you to do (in terms of numbers) if you've changed the stitch pattern or yarn gauge, just because you're having trouble figuring it out. With time, patience, and a little resourcefulness, you'll find that altering patterns is possible!

Starting a men's knitting group

Starting a community of male knitters in your area can be a helpful step towards sharing a craft you love while learning new techniques and hip new ideas from other crafters. Here are a few ideas to help you start your own.

Set a date and time—and stick with it. Before you put the word out to too large a group, get together your first members and choose a location and time to meet. Some groups meet every week—sometimes once a month or every other week. Be sure to pick a location that's convenient to group members and fits all the relevant criteria. Your location should be well lit, not so loud that conversation is impossible, and spacious enough to fit all your guys. Think about checking with the café, restaurant, or bar owner before you set the night. They might be able to suggest another night or location if it doesn't work well—or if it does, they might be willing to help you with promotion by advertising or setting menu specials!

Finding other guys in your area who knit

You might already know several, but it's a good idea to make a quick flyer and hang it anywhere you think other knitters might frequent—yarn and fabric stores are a good start, but don't be afraid to broaden your horizons to places like cafés, bookstores, or even hardware stores. All sorts of guys knit—and you might find a whole trove of them somewhere you wouldn't readily think to look.

Another way to attract other male knitters is to knit in public. While just knitting on the subway, you might meet someone who is learning to knit and has been looking for a group—or even another knitter whose boyfriend knits and has been looking for company.

Last but not least, check out all the online options. Websites like Craigslist and community listserves see a ton of traffic and can be a great way to get the word out.

Support beginners when they come to your group for the first time. The first time you came to a knitting group, it might have been a little hard because you didn't know anyone. The same is likely to be true for many newcomers—be sure to be polite and introduce yourself and other guys in the group.

Don't get frustrated if it takes a while for the group to get started. For every knitting group where I've been a founding father, it can take a few weeks to get the word out. The important thing is to come every week—and before you know it, your group will grow!

Men's knitting resources

Finding unique patterns for guys can be a bit of a challenge but keep your eyes open: you'll find there are some treasure troves of patterns, articles, and books—starting with these.

Websites

Menknit.net—The online resource for men who knit: discussion forums, a listing of male knitting blogs from around the globe, and a quarterly online mag with patterns and essays for (and often by) men.

MenWhoKnit.com—Promoting and inspiring knitting amongst men. The site serves as a "hub" for men's knitting blogs, offers information on monthly groups, and makes it easy to contact other men who knit.

Knitty.com—One of the first and most well-maintained online knitting mags. Updated quarterly, the site features patterns, articles, how-tos on difficult techniques, and all that's new and exciting. Their "man" issue (Summer 2005) has some hip and interesting patterns.

Books

Rowan, a UK-based yarn company and publisher, releases two coffee-table size issues per year. Earlier issues (check out No. 34) have sweater and accessory patterns for guys from fabulous designers such as Kaffe Fassett, Kim Hargreaves,

and Louisa Harding. Recent issues have included more vintage and unique design elements for guys.

Jaeger, another yarn company, also distributes pattern books each season. Though most designs are for women and children, the JB28 collection (2004) is devoted to men's patterns.

Sweater Design in Plain English by Maggie Righetti explains body shape, gauge, and has 20+ examples which explain how to think about design in relation to body size and intended recipient.

Glorious Knits, **Family Album**, **Kaffe's Classics** and others by Kaffe Fassett—one of knitting's first male designers, Fassett's collections use combinations of color in both Fair Isle and Intarsia to create unique and complex garments. Many are designed and sized for men; others are unisex.

Sweaters for Men, **Aran Knitting**, **Pacific Coast Highway** and others by Alice Starmore, though mostly out of print, feature more than a few stylish men's sweaters. Check your local library.

Handknitting and **Knitting** by Meg Swansen, daughter of Elizabeth Zimmermann, Meg picks up the torch of design and technique from her famed mother. Her books have a fair number of classic men's sweaters, and feature many of Zimmermann's techniques, which are a great resource for guys interested in expanding their knowledge of the craft into unexplored territory.

Yarn Company Info

Alchemy (Yarns of Transformation)
PO Box 1080
Sebastopol, CA 95473 USA
T: 707.823.3276
www.alchemyyarns.com

Artyarns (Luxury Handpainted Yarns)
39 Westmoreland Avenue
White Plains, NY 10606 USA
T: 914.428.0333
www.artyarns.com

Berroco
14 Elmdale Road
PO Box 367
Uxbridge, MA 01569 USA
T: 800.343.4948
www.berroco.com

Blue Sky Alpacas, Inc.
PO Box 387
St. Francis, MN 55070 USA
T: 888.460.8862
www.blueskyalpacas.com

S. R. Kertzer Limited (distributes Butterfly Super 10)
50 Trowers Road
Woodbridge, ON L4L 7K6 Canada
T: 800.263.2354
www.kertzer.com

Brown Sheep Company, Inc.
100662 County Road 16
Mitchell, NE 69357 USA
T: 800.826.9136
www.brownsheep.com

Cascade Yarns
1224 Andover Park East
Tukwila, WA 98188 USA
T: 800.548.1048
www.cascadeyarns.com

Dale of Norway (Dale of Norway Inc.)
N16 W23390 Stoneridge Drive, Suite A
Waukesha, WI 53188 USA
T: 262.544.1996
www.dale.no

Design Source Collection (distributes Manos del Uruguay)
PO Box 770
Medford, MA 02155 USA
T: 888.566.9970

Knitting Fever International (distributes Noro)
PO Box 336,
315 Bayview Avenue
Amityville, NY 11701 USA
T: 516.546.3600
www.knittingfever.com

Koigu Wool Designs
RR# 1, Williamsford
Ontario, N0H 2V0 Canada
T: 888-765-WOOL
www.koigu.com

Malabrigo Yarn
Gaboto 1277
11200, Montevideo, Uruguay
T: 786.866.6187
www.malabrigoyarn.com

Mountain Colors
4072 Eastside Highway
Stevensville, MT 59870 USA
T: 406.777.3377
www.mountaincolors.com

Peace Fleece
475 Porterfield Road
Porter, Maine 04068 USA
www.peacefleece.com

Westminster Fibers (distributes Rowan, Nashua Yarns)
4 Townsend West Unit 8
Nashua, NH 03603 USA
T: 603.886.5041
www.knitrowan.com

Stitch index

Take a look through the Stitch Index here—sampling some of the stitches used in this book—for inspiration on applying texture or style to a project of your own design as you progress in knitting.

Diamond brocade

(Multiples of 8 plus 1)

Row 1: (RS) K4 *P1 K7

rep from *, ending P1 K4.

Row 2: P3 *K1 P1 K1 P5 rep

from *, ending

last rep P3.

Row 3: K2 *P1 K3 rep

from *, ending last rep K2.

Row 4: P1 *K1 P5 K1 P1

rep from *.

Row 5: *P1 K7 rep

from *, ending P1.

Row 6: P1 *K1 P5 K1

P1 rep from *.

Row 7: K2 *P1 K3 rep

from *, ending last rep K2.

Row 8: P3 *K1 P1 K1 P5 rep

from *, ending

last rep P3.

Rep rows 1–8 for patt.

Twisted rib

(in the round)

(Multiples of 2)

Rnd 1: *K1tbl P1* to end.

Rep row 1 for patt

Swedish check

(Multiples of 4)

Note: All sts are slipped pwise.

Row 1: (RS) Sl 1, knit through

back loop (tbl) to last st, K1.

Row 2: Sl 1, purl to last st, K1.

Row 3: Sl 1 K2 tbl *P2 K2 tbl,

rep from * to last st, K1.

Row 4: Sl 1 P2 *K2 P2, rep

from * to last st, K1.

Row 5: Sl 1, knit tbl

to last st, K1.

Row 6: Sl 1, purl to last st, K1.

Row 7: Sl 1 P2 *K2 tbl P2,

rep from * to last st, K1.

Row 8: Sl 1 K2 *P2 K2, rep

from * to last st, K1.

Rep rows 1–8 for patt.

Basketweave

(Multiples of 16)

Row 1: *K8 P8 rep from *.

Rows 2–8: Rep row 1.

Row 9: *P8 K8 rep from *.

Rows 10–16: Rep row 9.

Rep rows 1–16 for patt.

Fisherman's rib A

(Multiples of 2)

Rnd 1: *P1 K1 in st below rep from *.

Rnd 2: *P1 K1 rep from *.

Rep rnds 1 and 2 for patt.

Reverse stockinette stitch

(in the round)

Rnd 1: Purl.

Rep rnd 1 for patt.

Linen stitch

(Multiples of 2 plus 3)

Row 1: (RS) K1 *Slip 1 pwise wyif K1 rep from * to end.

Row 2: P2 *Slip 1 pwise wyib P1 rep from * to end P1.

Rep rows 1 and 2 for patt.

3 x 3 rib

(in the round)

(Multiples of 3)

Rnd 1: *K3 P3 rep from *.

Rep rnd 1 for patt.

Ribbed check

(Even number of sts)

Row 1: *K1 P1 rep from *.

Row 2: *K1 P1 rep from *.

Row 3: *P1 K1 rep from *.

Row 4: *P1 K1 rep from *.

Rep rows 1–4 for patt.

Abbreviations

beg	beginning; begin; begins		**pwise**	purlwise
bet	between		**rem**	remaining
BO	bind off		**rep**	repeat, repeating
CC	contrast color		**rev St st**	reverse stockinette stitch
cn	cable needle		**rnd**	round
CO	cast on		**RS**	right side
cont	continue, continuing		**Sl**	slip
dec	decrease		**Sl m**	slip marker
dpn	double-pointed needle		**Sl 1 pwise**	slip one purlwise with
foll	following		**wyib**	yarn in back
ft.	feet		**Sl 1 wyib**	slip one with yarn in back
in.,"	inches		**Sl 1 wyif**	slip one with yarn in front
inc	increase		**SSK**	slip 2 stitches knitwise
K	knit			(one at a time); knit into
Kfb	knit front back			the front loops of the two
K2tog	knit 2 together			stitches together
kwise	knitwise		**st(s)**	stitch(es)
M	marker		**St st**	stockinette stitch
M1	make 1		**tbl**	through back loop
MC	main color		**work even**	continue in pattern without
mm	millimeter			increasing or decreasing
P	purl		**WS**	wrong side
patt	pattern		**yd.**	yard, yards
PM	place marker		**yo**	yarn over
PSSO	pass slipped stitch over		*** ***	repeat stitches between
P2tog	purl 2 together			the asterisks

Selected bibliography

Albright, Barbara (ed.). *Knitters Stash*. Interweave Press, 2001.

Budd, Ann. *The Knitter's Book of Handy Patterns: Basic Designs in Multiple Sizes and Gauges*. Interweave Press, 2002.

Budd, Ann. *The Knitter's Book of Sweater Patterns: Basic Designs in Multiple Sizes and Gauges*. Interweave Press, 2004.

Editors of *American Fabrics and Fashions Magazine*. *Encyclopedia of Textiles*, 3rd edn. Doric Publishing, 1980.

Editors of *Vogue Knitting Magazine*. *Vogue Knitting*. Pantheon Press, 1989.

Jenkins, Alison. *The Knitting Directory*. Prospero Books, 2004.

Le Court, Cynthia Gravelle. *Andean Folk Knitting: Traditions & Techniques from Peru & Bolivia*. Dos Tejedoras Fiber Arts Publications, 1990.

Maran Illustrated Knitting & Crochet. MaranGraphics, 2004–5.

Melville, Sally. *The Knitting Experience, Book 3: Color, The Power and the Glory*. XRX Books, 2005.

Righetti, Maggie. *Sweater Design in Plain English*. St. Martin's Press, 1990.

Rutt, Richard. *A History of Handknitting*. Interweave Press, 1987.

Starmore, Alice. *Aran Knitting*. Interweave Press, 1997.

Starmore, Alice. *Pacific Coast Highway*. Windfall Press for Broad Bay Company, 1997.

Stoller, Debbie. *Stitch 'N Bitch, The Knitters Handbook*. Workman Publishing, 2003.

Walker, Barbara G. *A Treasury of Knitting Patterns*. Schoolhouse Press, 1998.

Swansen, Meg. *Handknitting*. Schoolhouse Press, 1995.

Swansen, Meg, *Knitting*. Interweave Press, 1999.

Walker, Barbara G.. *A Second Treasury of Knitting Patterns*. Schoolhouse Press, 1998.

Wiseman, Nancie. *The Knitter's Book of Finishing Techniques*. Martingale & Company, 2002.

Zimmermann, Elizabeth. *Knitting without Tears: Basic Techniques and Easy-to-Follow Directions for Garments to Fit All Sizes*. Simon & Schuster, 1995.

Index

A

abbreviations 23
accessories 7, 29–76
afghans 112
Alchemy 62, 153
altering patterns 7, 144–47
American style 17
Aran 11, 52–55
Aran Pullover 108–11
Argyle Pullover Vest 96–100, 106
armholes 28

B

batch numbers 13
Beer Cozy 130–33
belts 34–37
binding off 22, 64, 130, 148–49
blankets 126
bobbins 106
books 152
Boot-Cut Sweater 84–89
boundoff seams 122
British Standard (BS) 12
Brunel, Marc 8
bulky yarns 11, 124
Business Card Holder 30, 33
buttons 78, 90, 119

C

cable cast-on 16
cable needles 10
Camo Coffee-Cup Cozy 48–50
care symbols 13
Cascade Pastaza 38
casting-off 22
casting-on 13–16, 129, 148–49
Casual Fridays Vest 78–83
Chardonnet, Hilaire de 8
charts 23, 102, 106, 128
Chiyareji Nitto: Otoka Amu 7
Chu'llu Hat and Scarf 58–61
circular needles 10, 43, 62, 65
coats 112–17
color 7, 11–12, 96, 101, 106–7,
    144–46
Continental style 17, 20–21, 51

Cotton Gin 8
cozies 7, 44–50, 130–33
customizing 143–50

D

decreasing stitches 26
definition 24
designing patterns 7
dictionaries 146–47
difficulty rating 6
Dog Tooth Throw 126–29
double cast-on 14
double knitting (DK) yarns 11, 124
double-pointed needles 10, 43, 132
duplicate stitch 96, 101
dyelots 13, 146

E

English Make 1 (M1) 26
English style 17–19, 51

F

Fair Isle 48–51, 58, 147, 152
Fassett, Kaffe 7, 152
felting 34, 37, 70, 134
fingering yarns 11, 146
finished measurements 23, 25
finishing 118–24
Fisherman's rib 42
Fisherman's Watchcap & Scarf Set
    38–47
floats 51
Fougner, Dave 7

G

garment construction 7, 144–45
garter stitch 84
gauge 11, 13, 23, 25, 147–50
German style 17
gloves 34, 47
groups 151
guilds 8

H

hand-eye coordination 6
Harding, Louisa 152
Hargreaves, Kim 152
hats 11, 14, 34, 38, 42, 58–61
heavy worsted yarns 11

Hiking Boot Socks 66–69
history 7–8
holders 11
holding the yarn 17–21
home gear 125–42
Hooded Alpaca Parka 90–94

I

increasing sleeves 150
increasing stitches 26
inspiration 145
Intarsia 51, 96, 102, 106–7, 152

J

jackets 7, 77–124
joining seams 122

K

Knee-Length Coat 112–17
Knit 2 Together (K2tog) 27
Knit Front Back (Kfb) 26
Knit NY 6
knit stitch 24
Knit Wallet 30–32
knit-on method 123
knitted cable 56–57
knitted cast-on 123
Knitter's Bible 146
knitting machines 8
knitting stitch 18
Koigu 70

L

labels 12–13, 25
lace yarns 11
lanolin 108
Laptop Cover 52–55
Lee, William 8
left-handedness 24
light worsted yarns 11
linen stitch 61
linings 134
long-tail cast-on 14–15
lot numbers 13

M

Madil 66
markers 10, 129
mathematics 148–50

measurements 144
Medallion cable 76
Medallion Mitts 28, 74–76
Melabrigo 96
men's knit nights 6
men's knitting groups 151
Mercer, John 8
merino 70, 96
midrow cast-on 123
Military Belt 34–37
mistakes 96, 101
mittens 11, 14, 28, 74–76
mohair 62
Moroccan Waistcoat 7
mufflers 62
Multi-media Cozy 43, 44–47

N
Nashua 126
needlepoint 101
needles 10, 13, 23–25
new balls 118
Norbury, James 7
Noro 112
Not-So-Rugged Scarf 62–64
notions 10–11, 23, 90, 134, 148

O
Osanu, Hashimoto 7

P
parkas 90–94
Patons 7
patterns 7, 23, 143–46, 148, 150
Percentage System 84
pickers 17, 51
picking-up stitches 28, 74, 129
picture knitting 106
projects 7–8, 11, 13
Purl 2 Together (P2tog) 27
purl stitch 19, 22, 24

R
rayon 8
resources 143, 152
rewriting patterns 148
Righetti, Maggie 152
ribbing 8, 22, 41, 42

right side (RS) 24–25
right-handedness 18, 24
row counters 10, 89
Rowan Calmer 78
rows per inch 25
Rutt, Richard 7

S
safety pins 11
Sandal Socks 70–73
scarves 7, 11, 16, 41–42, 58–64, 120
schematics 23, 83, 145, 148–49
scissors 11
seam allowances 120
selvedge stitches 120, 122–23
shade numbers 12
shaping 144–45, 149
shawls 11, 16, 120
Shetland wool 108
sleeves 28, 89, 149–50
slip knot 13
Slip Slip Knit (SSK) 27
slipped stitches 120
socks 7, 11, 14, 28, 34, 47, 66–73
Starmore, Alice 152
Steiner, Rudolph 6
stitches 7, 10–11, 23–25, 144, 146–47, 149
stitches per inch 25, 149
stockinette stitch 8, 13, 24, 38, 84, 147
stores 146, 151
straight needles 10
stranded knitting 51
Strutt, Jedediah 8
super bulky yarns 11
Swansen, Meg 152
swatches 25, 118, 144, 147
sweaters 7, 11, 16, 25, 28, 74, 77–124

T
tape measure 10
tapestry needles 10, 101
templates 150

tension 13, 17–18
texture 11, 144
three-needle bindoff 121
throwers 17
throws 120
tools 10–11
travel bag 7, 134–37
Treasury 146
Tribal Sweater 102–5
tricks 149
twisting yarn 107

U
Ultramerino 6 44
United Kingdom (UK) 7, 12
United States (US) 6, 13
utility cloth 7, 138–42

V
vests 7, 78–83
Vogue Knitting 7

W
Waldorf schools 6
Walker, Barbara 146
wallets 16, 30–32
washing socks 70
waterproofing 134
weaving ends 119
websites 13, 151–53
weights 11, 13, 124, 146
whipstitch 124
Whitney, Eli 8
wild oak cable 55
working in the round 47–50, 65, 130, 147–48
worsted yarns 11, 124
wrong side (WS) 24

Y
yarns 7, 11–13, 23–25, 118, 124, 145–47, 150–51, 153

Z
Zimmermann, Elizabeth 84, 145, 152
zippers 90, 95

Acknowledgments

To my mother and father—for turning me on to fabric glue, for helping me figure out a few uncooperative patterns, and for being supportive especially toward the end.

To Dan Vera—for inspiration on the Coffee Cup Cozy, for letting me talk to CBC Radio, and for being my rock at some low and near critical points.

To Witt Pratt—for answering questions early on, lending me books from his library, turning my creative juices on full blast, and for being so generous.

To Pat Williams—for her advice early on, and to Barbara Schaffer Bacon and Pam Korza—for being so patient with my schedule, and listening to me work through my process.

To Threadbear Fiber Arts—for putting up with more than a few phone calls in search of color and yarn recommendations.

To the Yarn Harlot—who pulled me out of a sticky situation and offered her help freely from the start.

To my friends at DK Publishing: Rachel Kempster, Nichole Morford, and others whom I met and got to know after this page was due to press—thanks for all your work and for being so excited from the outset.

To my friends at Ivy Press: Judith More, Emily Gibson, Caroline Earle, and others behind the scenes—who found me, were supportive throughout, and took on the challenge of working with an author across the big pond.

To Holly Daymude, Molly Bettridge, Genia Planck, Courtney Messenger, Marney Andersen, Witt Pratt and Christine Cornwell—who did quick work to get the beautiful samples for the spreads.

To Karen Frisa—who took such loving care in editing my patterns and sizing them.

And finally, to Kirsten Hilgeford, Courtney Patterson, Sarah Freeman, John Brinegar, Rob Sheavly, Susan Meyer, the boys at Juice Joint, and others too numerous to name—thank you.

Publisher/Packager acknowledgments

Thanks to the following for use of images:
Page 6: Getty Images (Stone+/David C. Ellis)

Thanks to the following for lending props or locations:
Baroma—Seaford (cafe)
The Rainbow—Lewes (cafe)
Bone—Lewes (tailor's dummy)
John Shaw at Shaw Harley Davidson—Lewes
The Marlborough, Brighton (pub/pool table)